Director, Centre for Studies in Risk and Regulation, Laura Jones
Director, Social Affairs Centre, Fred McMahon
Director, Education Policy, Claudia Rebanks Hepburn
Senior Research Economist, Joel Emes
Research Analyst, Shahrokh Shahabi-Azad
Research Economist, Chris Schlegel

Ordering publications

To order additional copies of this book, any of our other publications, or a catalogue of the Institute's publications, please contact the book sales coordinator:

via our **toll-free order line: 1.800.665.3558, ext. 580**
via telephone: 604.688.0221, ext. 580
via fax: 604.688.8539
via e-mail: sales@fraserinstitute.ca.

Media

For media information, please contact Suzanne Walters, Director of Communications:

via telephone: 604.714.4582
or, from Toronto, 416.363.6575, ext. 582
via e-mail: suzannew@fraserinstitute.ca

Website

To learn more about the Institute and to read our publications on line, please visit our web site at www.fraserinstitute.ca.

Membership

For information about membership in The Fraser Institute, please contact the Development Department:

via mail to: The Fraser Institute, 4th Floor, 1770 Burrard Street,
Vancouver, BC, V6J 3G7
via telephone: 604.688.0221 ext. 586
via fax: 604.688.8539
via e-mail: membership@fraserinstitute.ca.

In Calgary, please contact us
via telephone: 403.216.7175
via fax: 403.234.9010
via e-mail: paulineh@fraserinstitute.ca.

In Toronto, please contact us
via telephone: 416.363.6575
via fax: 416.601.7322.

Publication

Editing and design by Kristin McCahon and Lindsey Thomas Martin
Cover design by Brian Creswick @ GoggleBox.

Can the Market
Save Our Schools?

Can the Market Save Our Schools?

EDITED BY CLAUDIA R. HEPBURN

The Fraser Institute
Vancouver, British Columbia, Canada
2001

Canadian Cataloguing in Publication Data

Main entry under title:

Can the market save our schools?

Includes bibliographical references.
ISBN 0-88975-185-4

1. School choice. 2. School choice--Canada. 3. Privatization in education. 4. Privatization in education--Canada. I. Hepburn, Claudia Rebanks. II. Fraser Institute (Vancouver, B.C.)

LB2806.36.C36 2001   379.3   C2001-910880-X

Contents

About the Authors

LYNN BOSETTI
The Alberta Charter School Experience

Lynn Bosetti received her Ph.D. in Educational Policy and Administration from the University of Alberta. She is a Professor in Policy and Administration, who has served as Vice Dean of the Faculty of Education at the University of Calgary. Currently she is the Special Assistant to the Vice President (Academic), External Academic Relations. She has recently completed the final report *Canadian Charter Schools at the Crossroads* for the Society for the Advancement of Excellence in Education and published recent articles on charter schools in the *Alberta Journal of Educational Research* and the *Peabody Journal of Education*. The recipient of a SSHRC grant to examine parental choice and the search for community, she is organizing a national conference on the Paradox and Promises of School Choice in Canadian Schools.

ANDREW J. COULSON
Market Education and the Public Good

Andrew J. Coulson is the author of *Market Education: The Unknown History*, which compares school systems from around the world, from ancient times to the present, in order to discover which have served the public well, which have not, and why. A Senior Fellow of the Mackinac Center and the editor of the web site www.SchoolChoices.org, he has written for such newspapers as the *Wall Street Journal* and the *Seattle Times*, and for such journals as the *Education Policy Analysis Archives* and the *Journal of Research in the Teaching of English*.

CHESTER E. FINN, JR.
Reinventing Public Education via the Marketplace

Chester E. Finn, Jr. is John M. Olin Fellow at the Manhattan Institute and President of the Thomas B. Fordham Foundation, of which he is also a trustee. He is also a Distinguished Visiting Fellow at Stanford's Hoover Institution. From 1995 to 1998, he was a senior fellow of the

Hudson Institute, where he now serves as an Adjunct Fellow. From 1992 to 1994, he served as founding partner and senior scholar with the Edison Project. Mr. Finn serves on a number of boards, including the Centre for Education Reform, Project Achieve, and the Foundation for Teaching Economics, as well as the advisory boards of the National Association of Scholars, the Centre of the American Experiment, and Parents Raising Educational Standards in Schools. From 1988 to1996, he served as a member of the National Assessment Governing Board, including two years as its Chairman. He has written and co-authored many publications on educational issues. He is on leave from the faculty of Vanderbilt University, where he has been Professor of Education and Public Policy since 1981.

MICHAEL GAFFNEY
An Evaluation of New Zealand's Targeted Individual Entitlement Scheme

Michael Gaffney has been a researcher at the Children's Issues Centre, University of Otago, New Zealand, since 1995. He trained as an elementary school teacher and then worked as a tutor and researcher in what is now the School of Education at the University of Otago. Mr. Gaffney has researched a range of topics relating to families and children, including family transitions, children's television, information technology, early childhood education, and schooling. He has also worked for New Zealand's Education Review Office, which is responsible for ensuring that all schools and early childhood services meet national requirements and teach the curriculum. Now a board member of the school his own children attend, he chairs the management board of an early childhood centre.

JAY P. GREENE
A Survey of Results from Voucher Experiments:
Where We Are and What We Know

Jay P. Greene is a senior fellow at the Manhattan Institute for Policy Research. He has conducted evaluations of school choice programs in Milwaukee, Cleveland, and San Antonio, as well as studied the effects of school choice on integration and civic values. His work has been published in such books as *Learning from School Choice* (The Brookings Institution, 1998), such journals as *The Georgetown Public Policy Review*, *Catholic Education*, and *Education and Urban Society*, and such newspapers as the *Wall Street Journal*, the *Washington Post*, and the *Cleveland Plain*

Dealer. He received his doctorate from the Department of Government at Harvard University in 1995 and has taught at the University of Houston and the University of Texas.

ALPHONSO HARRELL
A Student's Perspective on School Vouchers

Alphonso Harrell is an eleventh grade student at the college prep school, Cathedral High School, one of the top schools in the state of Indiana. He maintains a solid 'B' average, is a top wrestler, and excels in rugby and football. Always a very bright child who was eager to learn, Alphonso began to lose interest in school in the second grade. He and his mother were told that he was an above average student, who just wasn't meeting his potential. His mother asked for extra work or any other help, but none was forthcoming. The following year, she applied for a tuition grant from The Educational CHOICE Charitable Trust, a privately funded charity that helps low-income families in Indianapolis afford tuition at private schools. With the help of CHOICE, Alphonso entered Holy Cross Central Catholic School, where he soon excelled in academics and sports. Today, his goal is to attend Notre Dame College.

CLAUDIA R. HEPBURN
Editor

Claudia Hepburn is the Director of Education Policy at the Fraser Institute. Working in the Institute's Toronto office, she is a frequent media conmmentator on education issues. She is the author of *The Case for School Choice: Models from the United States, New Zealand, Denmark and Sweden* (Fraser Institute, 1999) and of many articles on education policy, published in *Fraser Forum* and newspapers across Canada. Ms. Hepburn began her career as a teacher working in Hong Kong, Poland and England, and in the Ontario secondary school system. She has a B.A. in English from Amherst College in Massachusetts, and an M.A. and B.Ed. from the University of Toronto.

CAROLINE M. HOXBY
Analyzing School Choice Reforms
That Use America's Traditional Forms of Parental Choice

Caroline M. Hoxby is the Morris Kahn Associate Professor of Economics at Harvard University and a research fellow of the National Bureau of Economic Research, a non-partisan think tank. She received her Ph.D. from M.I.T. and has a graduate degree in economics from Oxford, where she studied as a Rhodes Scholar. Dr. Hoxby's teaching and research focus on the economics of education, the labour market, and local governments. Her recent work on K-12 education includes papers on private school vouchers, and private and public school choice. She is currently conducting an evaluation of how charter schools affect student achievement and the public schools around them. In other recent work, Caroline Hoxby has studied the growth of teachers' unionization and its effects on American schools. She has also examined school finance equalization cases and has advised several states on their school finance cases. She has analyzed how class size reductions affect student achievement and has testified for state governments and the federal government on the effects of class size reduction. Recently, she has investigated peer effects in elementary and secondary schools.

BARBARA LEWIS
A Parent's Perspective on School Choice

Barbara Lewis is a single mother whose three children have attended public and private schools in Indianapolis. When her eldest son was in the second grade he was very unhappy and his teachers failed to respond to her concerns about his education. Ms. Lewis heard about the Educational CHOICE Charitable Trust in Indianapolis, a privately funded charity that helps low-income families in Indianapolis afford tuition at private schools, and applied for a scholarship for Alphonso. Alphonso was awarded one and used it to attend a private Catholic school. After seeing the change in her son's attitude toward his new environment and the positive response from teachers and administration at the new school, she became an active supporter of CHOICE and has helped to establish a grass-roots parents' organization called FORCE (Families Organized for Real Choice in Education).

WILLIAM ROBSON
Education in Ontario: Breaking the Deadlock

William Robson is the Vice-President and Director of Research at the C.D. Howe Institute. While he specializes in Canadian fiscal and monetary policy, Mr. Robson is also active in education reform. He is a Director of the Organization for Quality Education, the Ontario Coalition for Education Reform, and the Society for the Advancement of Excellence in Education and also a past Chair of the Ontario Parent Council. He is a familiar media commentator and author of the book *Could Still Do Better* (1999), published by the Ontario Coalition for Education Reform. Mr. Robson has a B.A. from the University of Toronto and an M.A. from the Norman Paterson School of International Affairs at Carleton University.

ANNE B. SMITH
An Evaluation of New Zealand's Targeted Individual Entitlement Scheme

Professor Anne B. Smith is the director of the Children's Issues Centre at the University of Otago in Dunedin, New Zealand. She is an applied developmental psychologist with a particular interest in social development and in ecological and sociocultural influences on children's development. Anne's past research has been in the field of early childhood education and care. More recently she has incorporated children's own constructions of their experiences into a broad range of research studies.

JAMES TOOLEY
Serving the Needs of the Poor:
The Private Education Sector in Developing Countries

James Tooley is Professor of Education Policy at the University of Newcastle. Professor Tooley directed the study of private education investment opportunities in developing countries for the International Finance Corporation, the private finance arm of the World Bank, which led to his publication *The Global Education Industry* (IEA, 1999), now in its second edition. He has consulted for the IFC, World Bank (IBRD), UN, UNESCO, and Asian Development Bank Institute on private education in developing countries. In the UK, he has influenced education policy development and serves on the UK government's curriculum and assessment committee. He is a regular contributor to radio and television debates and a frequent keynote speaker at international conferences on educational issues. Since 1995 he has also directed the Education Program at the Institute of Economic Affairs. Professor Tooley is the author of numerous scholarly and popular articles on the role of government and the private sector in education, as well as several books and monographs, including *Reclaiming Education* (Cassell, 2000), *Education without the State* (IEA, 1996), *The Higher Education Debate* (IEA, 1997), *Educational Research: A critique,* (Ofsted, 1998) and *The Seven Habits of Highly Effective Schools* (TCT, 1999). Professor Tooley received his Ph.D. from the Institute of Education, University of London, and has held educational research positions at the Universities of Oxford and Manchester and the National Foundation for Educational Research. Prior to entering educational research and policy he was a mathematics teacher in Zimbabwe.

Acknowledgements

This book is the result of many people's work. First, I would like to thank the authors, eight of whom are well-known education scholars who have contributed years of research to this project. The other two authors offer insights gained from personal experiences with two systems of education, one a virtual monopoly and the other market-driven. I learned a tremendous amount from all ten. The authors worked independently, and their views do not necessarily represent those of The Fraser Institute, its board of directors, or its supporters.

I am also grateful to the book's reviewers, Jason Clemens and Stephen Easton, for questions and criticisms that have greatly improved the book. Thanks also to Laura Jones and Stephen Easton for their advice and encouragement throughout the project. As always, it was a pleasure to work with them.

The publication of *Can the Market Save Our Schools?* has been generously assisted by a grant from the W. Garfield Weston Foundation.

Introduction

This book considers the potential of market-based policies to address the problems facing Canadian education. It offers the results of systematic research into the effects that other market-based education reforms have had in Canada and around the world where they have been tried and tested, in some cases for years, in others for generations. The collected papers shed a timely light on the Ontario government's proposed refundable tax credit for independent schooling, a policy that is bound to encourage an education market in Ontario and set an example for the rest of Canada. Will such a market, in which parents choose schools and schools compete for students, be good for education? This book attempts to answer that question.

Can the Market Save Our Schools? is, in part, the product of a Fraser Institute conference, **School Choice: Dispelling the Myths and Examining the Evidence,** held in April 2000, at which international scholars reported an array of evidence on educational choice and its impact on children, schools, and school systems around the world. This volume contains seven papers from that conference and includes three more papers to elaborate some of the themes.

The purpose of this book is to study the potential of market-based solutions to address the problems facing Canadian education. It is divided into three sections. In the first section, **Can the Market Save Our Schools?** the authors consider the educational status quo in Canada and the United States, and then suggest why developing an educational market, where schools are allowed to compete more freely for students, will produce better educational results for more students. They suggest that the public's goals for its education system would be more attainable if we encouraged schools to respond to the demands of parents rather than to those of the bureaucracy. In the second section, **Case Studies in Market Education**, five respected academics contribute the results of their research on a range of market mechanisms, from traditional forms of school choice, to charter schools, vouchers, and choice for the poor in developing countries. And in the final section, **Grassroots Perspectives on Choice**, a parent and a student who have both used a voucher program comment on the differences between the non-market and market systems. Their anecdotal experience casts a very different light on the real effects of policy decisions made by those in comfortable offices, with multiple diplomas and adequate disposable income to choose the schools their own children attend.

Can the Market Save Our Schools?

In the first chapter, **Publicly Funded Education in Ontario: Breaking the Deadlock,** William Robson pinpoints the problems with education in this province: too little academic achievement and too much centralized power. Robson explains the problem of low academic achievement in a province that has eschewed objective assessment for a generation. As he shows, the trouble lies not so much in poor performance across the socioeconomic strata but more strikingly in the difference in achievement and literacy between poorer and wealthier students in this province.

If, as most people would agree, the *raison d'être* for public involvement with education is to provide equal opportunity for all children, then Ontario public schools are failing in their most important mission. Robson's findings underscore the gulf that separates the performance between low- and high- SES students in this province, and must come as a wake-up call to anyone who remains to be convinced about the need for an overhaul of the system.

Robson summarizes the problems of over-centralization, saying,

> Publicly funded education in Ontario has become more centralized over the years, and bottom-up pressure to improve is weak because parents, teachers, principals, and school communities have little power to improve achievement at their schools. This lack of local power creates a vicious circle... Because opportunities to make a difference at their schools are few and feeble, many parents, teachers, principals, and community members who would like to see better results turn off... Their disengagement reinforces central control and further exposes schools to the influences of weak curriculum, poor assessment, and the indifference towards academic objectives from many in positions of influence in the education system.

Ontario's proposed education tax credit has the potential to turn this vicious circle into a virtuous one by empowering disenfranchised parents to vote with their feet. This will, in turn, encourage public schools to try to reengage parents or risk losing them to other schools.

According to Chester E. Finn Jr., certain market mechanisms used in the United States are having an impact on both sides of this equation of engagement. **Reinventing Public Education Via the Marketplace** is a transcription of Finn's keynote address to the conference, and in it he outlines the promise charter schools hold for the satisfaction of parents and the reorienting and energizing of school boards.

Charter schools are publicly funded schools that have been granted a charter to educate students outside the bounds of a public school district, for so long as they live up to the goals set out in their charter. Paid on a per pupil basis, they are attended by students whose families choose them. Charter schools are prohibited from enrolling students selectively and usually take students on a first-come, first-served basis or by lottery. Charter schools were pioneered in Minnesota in 1991 and today more than 2,000 of the 80,000 public schools in the United States are charter schools. (In Canada, only Alberta currently has charter schools. See, for example, http://www.charterschools.ca/, the Canadian charter schools research site.)

Finn, who focuses his attention on the potential of charter schools to reinvigorate public education, describes four phases that school boards go through when they first meet and then become familiar with charter schools. At first school boards unanimously reject this new breed of schools. If legislation makes charters possible despite school board resistance, they do everything in their power to keep them few and weak. Most boards in the United States, Finn claims, are caught in one of these two first stages. Attitudes change by phase three when the schools start to recognize that charter schools are not the only ones that can provide varied curriculum, timetables, and extracurricular activities. And finally, school boards in different parts of the country are starting to experiment with their own charter schools and using the power of this market mechanism to improve the quality and variety of the education they offer.

Andrew Coulson, the author of **Market Education and the Public Good**, has spent five years studying the effect of different educational policies throughout history. When conducting his research, Coulson considered how similar educational systems operate in different cultural and historical settings, how different systems operate in similar settings, and the different outcomes that result when one society changes from one educational system to another. In this chapter he compares the social effects of a market system with those of government controlled educational systems, in an attempt to respond to the criticism that "if parents were completely free to decide the course of their children's education, our societies would be factionalized and balkanized, destroying social cohesion." Coulson makes his case for the superior social outcomes of market education by recounting, among others, the educational practices of Athens and Sparta in ancient Greece, the origins of Canada's public school system, the trouble behind the 19th century Bible riots of Pennsylvania, and the issues fomenting rancour among parents and educators in Ontario today. He concludes that

> time and again, heterogeneous societies have been able to exist in comparative harmony thanks to the freedom of parents to obtain the sort of education they value without forcing it on their neighbours. State school systems, by contrast, have consistently been used by powerful groups (whether democratic majorities or ruling elites) to discriminate against weaker groups.

These three, then, predict that market education will offer poor families greater educational equity, invigorate the state system, encourage parental involvement in their children's education, and foster social harmony.

Case Studies in Market Education

In the next section devoted to case studies academic researchers offer the results of their research on the effect market policies are currently having on other educational systems similar to our own. These papers assess the value of a spectrum of market policies: from choice among public school districts at one end to choice among public and private education providers at the other.

The first chapter in the second section looks at a case study whose subject is not only basic to the organization of North American public schools but also relevant to recent changes to Ontario's public system. Harvard economist Dr. Caroline Hoxby has sought to ascertain the value of school choice by studying the oldest form of school choice: choice among school districts and private schools.

As she points out in **Analyzing School Choice Reforms That Use America's Traditional Forms of Parental Choice**, two kinds of choice have always existed in the United States, as they have in Canada. Some cities have always had many school districts and many private schools, while others have only one school district and very few private schools.

This has resulted in a great difference in the amount of school choice available to parents, and Hoxby sets out to use these differences to answer three related questions. First, she asks, what can we learn about the relationship between these two traditional forms of school choice and such things as student achievement, school efficiency, teachers' salaries, and parental involvement? Second, how do those findings carry over to newer, market-style reforms such as open enrolment, charter schools, and voucher programs? And finally, what information is missing to predict accurately the effects of those newer reforms? Hoxby summarizes the results of her own inspired empirical research, published in several studies, to answer these questions and discuss their implications.

Among Hoxby's many fascinating findings is that "an increase in choice improves student achievement even while accomplishing substantial cost savings," which suggests choice has a potent impact on the productivity of schools. Not only does school productivity increase with school choice, but so does parental involvement. With school choice, school administrators are more likely to say that "parents have a more significant influence on school policy." These things are true, Hoxby says, whether the choices available to parents are among public districts or among private and public schools. But, "when parents have more choice within the public sector, they are more likely to be satisfied by their public options and less likely to choose private options."

Hoxby tells us that "evidence of what happens when an area has more choice among public school districts is useful ... for analyzing charter school reforms." In 1994, Alberta became Canada's first province to enact charter school legislation and today the province has nine charter schools. In 1996, Dr. Beverly Lynn Bosetti of the University of Calgary was charged with a three-year study of the outcomes and impact of Canada's charter schools. In this paper, **The Alberta Charter School Experience**, she outlines that study's findings, which corroborate Hoxby's evidence that a market of competing public schools is more effective than a single-district monopoly.

The next three papers move beyond the public school market and consider what happens when lower socio-economic status families can choose between public and private education providers. Wealthier families, of course, have always had this choice. They have been able to afford either to live in neighbourhoods with better public schools, or to pay for private school tuition. Poorer families have been more limited, both in their choice of residence and in their selection of schools.

Educational vouchers—tuition that follows the child to the parents' choice of school—are a means of making broader choices available to more families.

For decades academics and policy-makers have been divided on the value of private schooling. Some researchers have found that, after controlling for background differences, private school students have higher academic achievement than their public school peers. Other researchers have disagreed, claiming that certain ineffable differences between public- and private-school families, differences that are impossible to measure, are the real reason private school students appear to do better. As long as the research compared families who chose private schools with those who did not, this objection was unanswerable.

The last five years, however, have offered a reason to end the debate. Voucher programs have grown exponentially over the past decade, and some of them have been designed with the express purpose of answering this age-old question. In 1990, in the United States, the first government-funded voucher program started in Milwaukee and the first privately funded program was established in Indianapolis. Today, 68 privately funded programs serve 500,000 students, and 3 publicly funded programs offer choice to 12,000 students in cities and states across the US. The United States was certainly not the first country to experiment with this market mechanism. Britain had a voucher program for 16 years until 1996, which allowed bright low-income students to access private schools. Denmark has always made funding available to families who prefer independent schooling. Many Canadian provinces offer some funding to independent schools that meet certain criteria and regulations. In short, vouchers are neither new nor radical. They have been used in different ways by a wide variety of well-educated, thoughtful, and tolerant societies as a means of achieving the goals of public education. Private scholarships, on the other hand, have been used since ancient Greece as a means to increase the education levels of citizens and have become more numerous today in countries where monopolistic education systems have failed a large proportion of students.

Dr. Jay Greene, a chief researcher in several important American voucher studies, uses his chapter, **A Survey of Results from Voucher Experiments: Where We Are and What We Know**, to address three critical questions, which recent work on vouchers has helped answer. "What," he asks, "are the academic effects of school choice on families who choose their schools?... What are the academic effects of school choice on the public school system? And... what are the effects of school choice on the civic values and integration that we wish schools to promote?"

Perhaps, for those of us who get most of our information on these issues from television and the popular press, his most startling finding is that very little disagreement exists among researchers who have studied the effects of vouchers. All the researchers agree that families are overwhelmingly satisfied with the results of their voucher schooling and all of them endorsed school choice. None of the three major researchers found that vouchers harmed students. The two studies that relied on a rigorous "random assignment comparison found significant academic benefits from choice," while the less rigorous "non-random assignment comparisons found that choice did not significantly help or hurt students academically." As Greene concludes, "if these studies are mixed, as some are like to say, they are only mixed to the extent that they are positive or neutral on the effects of choice on test scores." On the usefulness of choice as a tool for poor families, the three researcher teams are unanimous in their support. He reminds us that "this is about as close as one gets to a positive consensus among researchers examining a controversial policy."

New Zealand started its own voucher program for low-income students as part of the government's broad effort to institute market reforms in the 1990s. In 1996, the Targeted Individual Entitlement (TIE) Scheme was established to "lift the educational achievement" of low-income families and make "it more likely that these families [would] get the kind of education that they want for their children" (NZMoE 1996, 2). Anne Smith and Michael Gaffney, researchers at the University of Otago, were charged with studying the success of the scheme from the perspective of children, parents, schools administrators, and teachers and to determine whether or not the program achieved the government's goals. Gaffney and Smith's paper, **An Evaluation of the TIE Scheme**, reiterates the success reported by Greene of voucher programs closer to home.

Though vouchers have proven to help low-income families in affluent societies access the educational resources of their wealthier neighbours, many people remain unconvinced about the power of the market to provide equal scholastic opportunities to the children of people who are themselves uneducated and impoverished. Perhaps, some critics say, vouchers will allow the children of bright, motivated, well-educated parents to access better schools, but what about the vast majority of lower SES families? They lack the skills to choose good schools and the motivation to keep their children in them.

James Tooley, a professor of Education Policy at Britain's University of Newcastle, addresses this recurring objection in this section's final chapter, **Serving the Needs of the Poor: The Private Education Sector in Developing Countries**. Tooley questions public education's record of service to the poor and, summarizing research from some of the world's poorest countries, contrasts it with the record of private education for the poor. He calls the belief still held by many that government schools can provide equity "a touching faith," considering the evidence.

Tooley cites research from Thailand, India, Colombia, the Dominican Republic, the Philippines, and Tanzania, all of which demonstrate that, after controlling for bias from social background, private schools are "more effective and less costly" than their state-run counterparts. Most interesting, though, is his own field work on private education entrepreneurs in India.

Tooley tells one story about an Indian company, NIIT, that with over 1,000 franchised and 40 wholly-owned IT training centres across India "embodies much of the excitement and innovation in the education industry." Like any well-run business, NIIT invests in research and development, and the company has recently studied how to reach the large population of illiterate and unschooled children through the Internet.

The research team set up an "Internet kiosk" in the boundary wall of their office block, which bordered on a slum area. A computer monitor, visible through a window, had a dedicated connection to the Internet and was accessible to anyone outside through an unbreakable joystick. No announcement was made about the kiosk and no instruction was provided, but activity was monitored by NIIT.

Within a very little time the kiosk became a favourite among local children. Their favourite sites were the Disney Web site, news, horoscopes, short stories, and Paint, through which children who normally would have had no access to paper learned to draw and write their names. Tooley writes,

> The observations thus far indicate that underprivileged children from the slum area, without any planned instructional intervention, could achieve a remarkable level of computer literacy. The experiment suggests that language, technical skills, and education are not serious barriers to accessing the Internet, and, through it, educational and

entertainment CD ROMs. It also suggests that the Internet can lead to self- and peer-education—at least for younger children. Over the age of 14 or so, people didn't make much sense of it at all: 'Where's the teacher?' they would ask.

NIIT, Tooley reports, "is now embarking on marketing the idea to rural and slum areas, harnessing the power of the private sector to reach the poorest through modern technology." The virtual school will have reached Indian slums without any government intervention long before it becomes a reality in Canada.

Grassroots Perspectives on Market Mechanisms

The last two chapters are really more of a coda to this academic book than an equivalent final section. In **Grassroots Perspectives on Market Mechanisms**, I have transcribed the two final speeches from last April's conference. According to some in the audience, these anecdotal stories from two Americans have little or no relevance to Canadian education policy-makers. According to others, Barbara Lewis and Alphonso Harrell offered the most compelling evidence they had heard all day. I include them for the reader to decide.

Whatever their intrinsic merit, these stories bring the book full circle. Ms. Lewis's problems with the Indianapolis public school system are exactly those described by Mr. Robson with regard to Ontario education: "Because opportunities to make a difference at their schools are few and feeble, many parents, teachers, principals, and community members who would like to see better results turn off." Fortunately for Ms. Lewis and her son, a voucher program was available and she did not "turn-off." Instead she moved her son to a better school and became *more* involved in her children's education. Not only did the voucher encourage her to find schools that would teach them academic skills and discipline, it also encouraged her to become a leader in education reform in her state. She and Alphonso are two examples of how one market policy can transform Robson's vicious circle into a virtuous one of engaged citizenry, responsive schools, and well-educated young people. They are living, breathing, *thinking* proof of how the market can save our schools.

Taken as a whole, these chapters suggests that Ontario's controversial tax credit, which will make independent schooling accessible to the majority of families in the province, is a wise policy. If the evidence is to be believed, the reform will improve educational outcomes both for the children who take advantage of it, and for those who do not.

Those who, having read this book, remain unconvinced by it may at least agree that Canadians, like the Indian businessmen running NIIT, can only improve the education available to children if they test the effects of promising new education policies. Only then will Canada have its own answer to the question, *Can the Market Save Our Schools?*

—CLAUDIA R. HEPBURN

SECTION ONE:
Can the Market Save Our Schools?

Publicly Funded Education in Ontario: Breaking the Deadlock

WILLIAM ROBSON
Director, Ontario Coalition for Education Reform and
Vice-President and Director of Research, C.D. Howe Institute

Introduction and Overview

Ensuring that young people get the necessary knowledge and skills for an independent, fulfilling existence is one of life's most important tasks. Educating one's own children is a hallmark of a good parent. And trying to provide an education for children whose families are unable or unwilling to take on that task has inspired systems of state-supported education in every liberal democracy.

Ontarians have for decades made enormous commitments to publicly-funded education. We vie with anyone, not only for verbal support, but also in resources invested.[1] Yet our achievements, though perhaps impressive in the past, are not commensurate with our commitments.

The Problem: Underperformance and Overcentralization

Student achievement in Ontario is, on average, unimpressive compared to objective standards and achievement elsewhere. More strikingly, the

I thank John Bachmann, Dave Cooke, Cathy Cove, Malkin Dare, Mark Holmes and Yanhong Zhang for comments, and absolve them of responsibility for the opinions expressed here and for any remaining errors.

wide dispersion of achievement scores and the high proportion of students in programs related to academic incapacity suggest that the key goal of publicly funded education—ensuring that all young people start adult life with at least a basic level of competence—is not being achieved.

There are many plausible suspects behind this failure. My list includes incomplete curriculum, inadequate assessment, and a culture among many education professionals that ranks academic achievement behind the inculcation of politically correct attitudes and self-esteem. These flaws matter. Similar problems afflict other education systems, however, and the consequences are not always as serious. In Ontario, something seems to make us more vulnerable to challenges that jurisdictions where achievement is higher and less dispersed—such as Alberta, Quebec, and many continental European countries—appear to confront more successfully.

In my view, Ontario's inability to overcome these handicaps stems largely from dysfunctional governance. Publicly funded education in Ontario has become more centralized over the years, and bottom-up pressure to improve is weak because parents, teachers, principals, and school communities have little power to raise achievement at their schools.

This lack of local power creates a vicious circle, moreover, producing the deadlock referred to in my title. Because opportunities to make a difference at their schools are few and feeble, many parents, teachers, principals, and community members who would like to see better results turn off, and devote their time and energy to more promising causes. Their disengagement reinforces central control, and further exposes schools to the influences of weak curriculum, poor assessment, and the indifference toward academic objectives on the part of many in positions of influence in the education system.

The Solution: Bottom-Up Pressure for Improvement

If this diagnosis of the problem is correct, the cure lies in measures that will strengthen bottom-up pressure to improve. We need to give individual schools more autonomy. And we need to ensure that competitive pressures created by expanded parental choice will give more autonomous schools incentives to use that autonomy to improve student achievement.

School councils could provide a platform for school-based governance in the future, and charter schools are a model Ontario could usefully follow to create more school autonomy. When it comes to incentives, new funding arrangements that empower parents to seek out the best schools for their children would be a powerful force for bottom-up improvement, with partial funding for independent schools being another cost-effective option.

Lack of interest on the part of the provincial government and opposition from many vested interests in the public-education industry may make early progress along these lines unlikely. In that case, privately financed vouchers would be invaluable for the students who used them, and a useful prod to improvement for the system as a whole.

Student Achievement in Ontario

To many people, the statement that Ontario's publicly funded elementary and secondary schools underperform would appear so uncontroversial as to need little backing up. But partly because the system resisted objective assessment for decades, there has been a lot of scope for contrary views, so it is worth spending a moment looking at the evidence.

Poor Average Student Achievement

Although no one has systematically surveyed the situation, testimony from post-secondary instructors suggests that the rise in post-secondary enrolment rates is uncovering major failings in the elementary and secondary school systems. Complaints about the increasingly unprepared state of incoming students are widespread. First-year remediation is already a major industry in community colleges, and may soon be one in universities as well (Robson et al. 1999, 7-9).

Complaints from post-secondary instructors are reinforced by evidence of Ontario's weak performance relative to other jurisdictions. International tests have shown Ontario in an unfavourable light for years.[2]

The 1995 Third International Mathematics and Science Study (TIMSS), the most ambitious comparison yet, confirmed this pattern. Among the 17 countries providing comparable data for grade 4 students, Canada placed eighth in math and sixth in science. Adding to the rankings the five provinces—British Columbia, Alberta, Ontario, New Brunswick, and Newfoundland—that oversampled to allow independent comparison put Ontario eleventh in science, trailing every other province except New Brunswick, and thirteenth in math, last among the provinces.[3] Treating the 5 provinces independently again, TIMSS produced comparable results for grade 8 students for 31 jurisdictions: Ontario scored 18th in math, behind every province but New Brunswick, and 22nd in science, last among the provinces (and behind the United States).

Particularly worrisome is that Ontario (like the United States) stood out for relatively meagre improvement from grade to grade: students in higher grades were further behind their peers abroad. Between grades 7 and 8, Ontario students improved their math performance by less than most other jurisdictions, and their improvement in science was second lowest (author's calculations from data in Robitaille, Taylor and Orpwood 1997).[4] Defenders of Ontario education often claim that these tests fail to control for differences in student coverage and curriculum. A review of the TIMSS results for Ontario's Education Quality and Accountability Office (EQAO), however, found that the top achieving countries tested a higher proportion of their students than Ontario did, and that rankings based only on responses on topics covered in the Ontario curriculum were the same as the overall rankings (Orpwood 1998, 5).

Inter-provincial tests confirm the message that, within Canada, Ontario is a laggard. The 1997 School Achievement Indicators Program (SAIP) tests in mathematics show Ontario's anglophone 13-year-olds and 16-year-olds to be middle-of-the-pack at best, and Ontario's francophones to be consistently among the bottom performers.[5] The difference between the scores from the two age groups, moreover, shows unimpressive relative improvement during the intervening years, with the francophone students' relative decline in the national rankings standing out.

In the 1996 SAIP science tests, Ontario's results were uniformly poor. Anglophone students were fifth from the bottom among 17 identified jurisdictions at age 13 and again at age 16.[6] Francophones were second last at both ages.

The 1994 SAIP results in reading also told a grim story. Judging from the proportion of students achieving level 3 or better on the SAIP's five-point scale, Ontario's anglophone 13-year-olds did reasonably well, though falling short of their counterparts in Alberta and Quebec. But the 16-year-olds slipped to the lower half of the pack, suggesting relatively little improvement in early high school. The same pattern was evident in writing: anglophone 13-year-olds did quite well (unlike their francophone counterparts) but 16-year-olds were below the middle of the pack, with a ranking by the difference in performance at the two ages putting Ontario dead last.

The results from the 1998 SAIP for reading and writing present a brighter picture in some respects. Ontario's anglophone 13-year-olds and 16-year olds both scored comparatively well in writing. In reading, the 16-year-old anglophones also did relatively well. Unfortunately, the good news did not extend to the francophone students, who ranked below the middle of the pack in reading and close to the bottom in writing at both ages (EQAO 1999, 72-73).

To help judge whether the 1998 SAIP anglophone results indicate a turnaround in Ontario's performance, one would ideally want consistent achievement tests over time. Unfortunately, since the abandonment of high-school exit exams over three decades ago, there has been almost no controlled testing in the province, so little information of this type exists. In the 1994-95 International Adult Literacy Survey (IALS), Ontarians aged 26 to 65 handily outperformed the rest of the country, surpassing even the strong-performing western provinces in two of the three categories tested, but Ontarians aged 16 to 25 underperformed the national average in all categories, scoring well below the west and also below Quebec (SC/CMEC 1999, 89). Although many factors other than school quality affect those results, they are consistent with relative deterioration.

Sporadic math tests in the early 1990s showed discouraging results (MET 1992a; 1992b; 1992c), and subsequent rounds inspired charges that administrators were lowering the bar to improve the story (Lewington and Orpwood 1993, 151-52). A 1994 test of grade 9 reading and writing made special accommodations for, or exempted, many weaker students, yet found that over half scored below "competent" on a six-point scale (see Daly 1994; Lewington 1994).

A new provincial testing agency, the EQAO, began testing grade 3 students in 1997 and is gradually extending its assessments to other grade levels. The results of its program to date are hard to interpret, for several reasons. The tests de-emphasize elements that are easy to score objectively, such as short-answer or multiple choice, in favour of constructed responses that are harder to grade consistently.[7] High proportions of students—around one-third of those in the grade 3 tests—receive special accommodations such as extra time or help in reading the questions, moreover, while several incidents have pointed to inadequate controls over writing conditions. Most important, the content of the tests is changing in response to past difficulties and the introduction of

Table 1   Students At or Above the Provincial Standard in EQAO Tests (percent)[8]

		1997	1998	1999	2000
Grade 3	Reading	50	46	44	49
	Writing	39	49	51	52
	Math	33	43	56	57
Grade 6	Reading	n.a.	n.a.	48	50
	Writing	n.a.	n.a.	48	48
	Math	n.a.	21	46	51
Grade 9	Math	n.a.	25	n.a.	n.a.
Grade 10	Literacy	n.a.	n.a.	n.a.	61

a new provincial curriculum. For what they are worth, however, the tests show that the proportion of students reaching or exceeding the provincial standard is not much better than half, and often well below it (Table 1).

Although the unsettled nature of these tests makes comparisons over time impossible, a 1997 pilot math test of grade 6 students duplicated some questions from a 1989 provincial math test and found that over the eight-year interval, the proportion of correct answers in number sense and numeration had dropped from 79 to 73 percent, and in measurement from 70 to 65 percent.[9]

Relatively Dispersed Student Achievement

The dispersion of achievement scores in Ontario is perhaps the most disconcerting evidence of failure to fulfill the ideals of publicly funded education. Socio-economic status and educational outcomes are correlated everywhere, but the link in Ontario is especially tight. Research has found that in Ontario there is a larger gap between the achievement of higher- and lower-socio-economic status students than there is elsewhere (Willms 1997). The differences between students from less and more promising socio-economic backgrounds in grade 7 and 8 math scores in TIMSS, for example, were greater in Ontario than elsewhere in Canada. Also, the link between socio-economic status and adult literacy in the IALS was far stronger in Ontario than in Quebec and the

Figure 1 SES Gradients for Youth, 1994 IALS

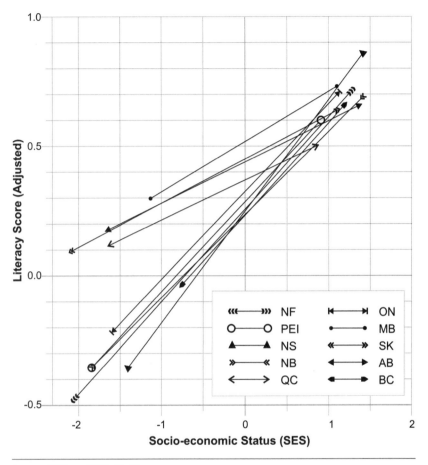

Source: Willms 1997, 19-21

prairies, where less advantaged young people scored closer to average than to less advantaged Ontarians (Figure 1).

A particularly disconcerting indicator in this context is the share of students that the new provincial tests miss—students who are exempted from the tests altogether, or whose results fall into the "no data" and "not enough information to score" categories. In the grade 3 reading tests, for example, 12 percent of students fell into these categories province-wide. And these no-results rates varied greatly from board to board: in 16 boards the exclusion rate was 15 percent or higher, and in three boards, it was 20 percent or higher. Table 2 provides two

Table 2 Students Missed in 1999/2000 EQAO Grade 3 Reading Test

Ranked by Shares	%	Ranked by Numbers	#
Northeastern Catholic DSB	24	Toronto DSB	2520
Superior North Catholic DSB	21	Toronto Catholic District School Board	940
Keewatin-Patricia DSB	20	Ottawa-Carleton DSB	690
Nipissing-Parry Sound Catholic DSB	19	Thames Valley DSB	600
DSB Ontario North East	19	Dufferin Peel Catholic DSB	580
Rainy River DSB	19	Simcoe County DSB	560
Hastings and Prince Edward DSB	17	Durham DSB	550
Kenora Catholic DSB	16	Waterloo Region DSB	540
Near North DSB	16	Peel DSB of Education	500
Huron-Superior Catholic DSB	16	Hamilton-Wentworth DSB	490
Northwest Catholic DSB	16	York Region DSB	460
Rainbow District School Board	15	Kawartha Pine Ridge DSB	420
Algoma DSB	15	Upper Canada DSB	380
Grand Erie DSB	15	Grand Erie DSB	330
Upper Canada DSB	15	Hamilton-Wentworth Catholic DSB	330
Hamilton-Wentworth Catholic DSB	15	DSB of Niagara	320
Catholic DSB of Eastern Ontario	14	Greater Essex County DSB	300
Kawartha Pine Ridge DSB	14	Ottawa-Carleton District Catholic School Board	290
Superior-Greenstone DSB	14	Halton DSB	280
Bruce-Grey Catholic DSB	14	Hastings and Prince Edward DSB	230
Limestone DSB	14	York Catholic DSB	230
Simcoe County DSB	14	Limestone DSB	230
Toronto DSB	13	Durham Catholic DSB	230
Peterborough Victoria Northumberland and Clarington CDSB	13	Hamilton-Wentworth Catholic DSB	220
Brant Haldimand Norfolk Catholic DSB	13	Lambton Kent District Public School Board	220
Waterloo Region DSB	13	Wellington Catholic DSB	210
Toronto Catholic District School Board	13	Bluewater DSB	200
Lakehead DSB	13	Windsor-Essex Catholic DSB	190

Board	Value
Ottawa-Carleton DSB	13
Algonquin and Lakeshore Catholic DSB	13
Greater Essex County DSB	12
Bluewater DSB	12
Wellington Catholic DSB	12
Renfrew County DSB	12
Hamilton-Wentworth DSB	12
Avon Maitland DSB	12
Durham DSB	12
Renfrew County Catholic DSB	11
Hamilton-Wentworth Catholic DSB	11
Lambton Kent District Public School Board	11
Durham Catholic DSB	11
Trillium Lakelands DSB	11
Windsor-Essex Catholic DSB	10
DSB of Niagara	10
Dufferin Peel Catholic DSB	10
St. Clair Catholic District School Board	10
Thames Valley DSB	10
Thunder Bay Catholic DSB	10
Simcoe Muskoka Catholic DSB	10
Halton Catholic DSB	10
Ottawa-Carleton District Catholic School Board	10
London District Catholic School Board	9
Huron-Perth Catholic DSB	9
Halton DSB	9
York Region DSB	8
York Catholic DSB	7
Upper Grand DSB	7
Sudbury Catholic DSB	7
Waterloo Catholic DSB	6
Peel DSB of Education	6

Board	Value
Upper Grand DSB	180
Halton Catholic DSB	170
Avon Maitland DSB	170
Trillium Lakelands DSB	160
Rainbow District School Board	160
Simcoe Muskoka Catholic DSB	160
Near North DSB	160
Catholic DSB of Eastern Ontario	160
Peterborough Victoria Northumberland and Clarington CDSB	150
London District Catholic School Board	140
Algoma DSB	140
Lakehead DSB	130
Algonquin and Lakeshore Catholic DSB	130
DSB Ontario North East	120
Waterloo Catholic DSB	100
Brant Haldimand Norfolk Catholic DSB	100
St. Clair Catholic District School Board	100
Renfrew County DSB	100
Huron-Superior Catholic DSB	100
Keewatin-Patricia DSB	100
Northeastern Catholic DSB	90
Thunder Bay Catholic DSB	80
Nipissing-Parry Sound Catholic DSB	70
Renfrew County Catholic DSB	60
Sudbury Catholic DSB	50
Rainy River DSB	50
Bruce-Grey Catholic DSB	40
Huron-Perth Catholic DSB	40
Superior-Greenstone DSB	30
Northwest Catholic DSB	20
Superior North Catholic DSB	20
Kenora Catholic DSB	20

perspectives on this problem: one panel ranks boards by the proportion of students for whom no result was recorded in reading; the other ranks them by the number of students for whom no result was recorded.[10] Given that the vast majority of the students for whom there were no results were exempted from the test or failed to produce interpretable results, it is likely that most of them would do poorly if they were tested. The system's failure to monitor their progress bodes ill for their catching up with their fellows before they either graduate or drop out.[11]

Why Low and Widely Dispersed Achievement Matters

Low average levels of achievement are highly worrisome, as is the fact that public schools in Ontario are doing less well at providing a common starting-line in life for the less advantaged.

In terms of economic considerations, it is well known that the dispersion of earned incomes in Canada has tended to increase since the early 1970s. Searches for the cause of rising inequality in earned incomes tend not to find convincing evidence for plausible culprits such as freer trade and technological change, leading some to speculate that the schools are not preparing many students for work life as well as they once did (Kuhn 1998, p. 374-375). Cross-country research suggests that countries in which students' scores on achievement tests are more unequal also tend to show greater dispersion of wage income among those age cohorts later in life (Bedard and Ferrall 1997).

Public Opinion

Public opinion surveys show recognition that the situation in Ontario's publicly funded schools leaves a lot to be desired. Since 1986, the share of respondents to Angus Reid surveys saying the quality of education was worse than it was 25 years ago has gone from 36 to 45 percent, while the proportion saying it was better fell from 42 to 26 percent. In 1996, barely more than half (53 percent) of Ontarians polled by Angus Reid said they were very or somewhat satisfied with public education in the province (ARG 1999); by 2000, that share had dropped to 43 percent. Tellingly, satisfaction was 10 percentage points lower (at 36 percent) among low-income Ontarians than it was among their high-income counterparts (ARG 2000).

Figures on relative enrolment growth also tell a convincing story. From 1987/88 to 1998/99, the average annual increase in regular public school enrolment was 0.9 percent. In publicly funded Catholic schools, the equivalent figure was 2.3 percent. Meanwhile, private school enrolment rose 3.5 percent per year: more than 90,000 students (4 percent of the total) now attend private schools, up from just over 60,000 in 1987/88.[12] And home schooling has grown explosively, from a negligible number in the 1980s to possibly 5,000 now.[13]

Funding and Governance

These indications of dissatisfaction prompted attention from both the NDP provincial government in the early 1990s and the Progressive Conservative government that replaced it in 1995. These governments took several steps intended to improve the system's performance, including a new curriculum, the reinstatement of testing, a new funding formula, and the amalgamation of school boards. The common theme behind these reforms was centralization. Provincial bodies now exert more influence than they did a decade ago. These bodies include most notably the Ministry of Education and Training, but also the Education Quality and Accountability Office (EQAO), the task force that oversaw school-board amalgamation, the Education Improvement Commission (EIC), and the newly established Ontario College of Teachers.

Another area of major change has been funding. Reforms in 1997 followed trends in other jurisdictions: a per-student funding formula that attempts to take into account such diverse considerations as educational needs, physical plant, and transportation. The intent was both to provide more equal amounts for students across the province than under the earlier system where school boards had access to the municipal tax base and, more important from the government's point of view, to try to force boards to cut spending on overheads.

The structure and functioning of school boards has changed in more ways than simply financial. Ontario's boards have now gone through yet another round of amalgamation. Thanks to amalgamation and amplified regulatory powers for the minister of education, elected school-board trustees have lost power.

The Deadlock: Limits to Top-Down Reform

Better performance is far from guaranteed, however, and there are important reasons for doubting that, on balance, further centralization of Ontario's education system is going to achieve it. Locating more levers of power in the Ministry of Education does not necessarily mean that they will be used well, or indeed that they will be used at all.

Ontario's education officials are notorious for ignoring the conclusions that years of research have led to concerning effective pedagogy. One example concerns the teaching of reading. Despite generations of evidence on the superiority of phonics over other methods of learning to read (Chall 1967; Adams 1989; Foorman et al., 1998; Watson and Johnson 1998; Robertson 1999), phonics instruction is absent from many classrooms. When the Canadian Psychological Association called for more use of phonics in reading instruction in 1992, the response from ministries of education was dismissive or hostile (CPA 1992).

What research shows to be effective is often loosely if at all connected to common practice—the superior results from teacher-directed instruction over child-centred learning (Engleman et al. 1988; American Institutes for Research 1999);[14] full-year versus semestered programs;[15] the importance of homework marked by teachers rather than by peers (EQAO1998, 6); and the healthier learning climate in small versus large schools (Coleman 1994, 34). These examples and others like them exist in many public education systems. They reflect the fact that, among administrators of these systems, academic achievement is only one objective among many, and often not a particularly high one. Under those circumstances, centralized control over program delivery may hurt, rather than enhance, the effectiveness of classroom practice.[16] There is, in short, no reason to assume that the additional levers of power now installed at Queen's Park will be used in ways that will enhance achievement.

Indeed, there is no reason to assume that many of these levers will be used at all. I have already referred to the large average exclusion rates in the EQAO's tests, and to the variation in those rates from board to board. This abdication of responsibility to monitor and account for the performance of less able students ought to be a scandal but, to the best of my knowledge, there have been no consequences of any kind for the administrators responsible.

This uneven commitment to student achievement makes it unlikely that a central push to raise the achievement of Ontario's students will be successful. Since average achievement levels are not impressive and the situation of many less advantaged students is bleak, this is an unsatisfactory prospect. Those seeking a better performance from Ontario's schools need to relinquish the hope that centralist reforms will provide it, and instead consider reforms that would unleash pressure from the bottom up.

Unleashing Bottom-Up Pressure to Improve Education

Provided that provincial standards and consistent measurement of achievement against those standards exist or are on their way, there are two ingredients to any bottom-up strategy. On the one side, schools need autonomy to improve their practice without direction from above, and sometimes in opposition to it. On the other, all parents—not just those with greater financial resources or the ability to make extraordinary sacrifices—need empowering to choose among schools, so that effective schools are rewarded with rising enrolments and funding, and less effective schools feel pressure to improve. School autonomy and parental empowerment separately may do some good: together, they could revolutionize Ontario's publicly funded schools.

School-Based Governance

When it comes to school autonomy, Ontario's education system currently divides into sharply contrasting categories. Independent schools operate quite freely: they are subject to health and safety regulations and occasional inspections, but one legacy of many years of weak provincial standards and no testing is an unclear mandate for the inspections. Publicly funded schools, by contrast, have little autonomy: principal selection is a board function; staffing decisions are largely circumscribed by board-union agreements; and budget-allocation and purchasing are largely controlled by the province and board-union agreements. Some boards have established schools with distinctive programs and pedagogical styles, but these schools have no independent standing and can be changed or abolished at a board's discretion.

Since the late 1980s, there has been sporadic interest in following steps elsewhere toward more effective school-level governance. The NDP government mandated school councils—bodies consisting of elected representatives of parents, teachers, non-teaching staff, community members, and (in some schools) students—in the mid-1990s, and the Conservative government legislated them in Bill 160.

To date, however, this initiative has been purely symbolic. Councils are advisory only, and there are no requirements for principals or boards to demonstrate that they listen to councils' advice or even to ensure they exist. A review of the situation of school councils by the EIC in 1998 recommended that they should remain powerless (EIC 1998). As the Ontario Parent Council has warned, this situation creates a vicious circle of disillusionment among originally enthusiastic council members, followed by disengagement. If councils' performance deteriorates as a consequence, this route to school-level governance could turn out to be a dead end (OPC 1998).

An optimist could make a case that the movement for greater autonomy of publicly funded schools will gain ground in the next few years. Bill 160 removed principals and vice-principals from the teacher unions. If British Columbian experience is a guide, their changed status may encourage principals to look to their local schools for support that they cannot obtain from boards or teachers. Some boards are soliciting the input of councils in principal selection. The Ministry of Education is now surveying council activity and members' views, apparently inspired by a desire to make involvement on councils more effective and rewarding.

This seems unlikely. Board amalgamation increased the distance between individual schools and board representatives. In the biggest board in the province, Toronto, local consultation on principal selection and staff-class allocations in elementary schools existed before amalgamation, but disappeared in its wake. Past Ministry and EIC initiatives around school councils have yielded boilerplate statements about the value of parental involvement and local input, but no substantive change.

The problem is not lack of effective ideas. It would be possible, for example, to design a system allowing councils that wished extra powers, all the way to principal selection, to take them up, while leaving those happy as they are unchanged (OPC 1998). The most recent OISE/UT survey found that more than one third of Ontarians favour giving councils the power to hire and fire principals. Since it is unlikely that the distribution of opinion across the province is uniform, probably in some schools, solid majorities would wish such powers (Livingstone et al, 2000). The problem is that the bulk of the players at the provincial level—politicians and bureaucrats alike—are comfortable with the status quo, and have little sympathy with a decentralized system that might be harder to control.

Many advocates of more local control look enviously at the explosion of charter schools in the United States and at Alberta, where charter schools have been operating since 1995. The rapid spread of US charters in areas where regular public schools were failing dismally—particularly poor inner-city neighbourhoods—shows how the pressure to empower parents (and teachers) badly served by the existing system can overcome the opposition of teacher unions and board bureaucrats.[17] Now that most US states have chartering laws, templates are available off the shelf. Alberta's experience provides further evidence of the demand for charter schools—evident in both the satisfaction of parents whose children attend them and long waiting lists—as well as home-grown lessons about how to design charter legislation (Bosetti et al. 2000). Much of what chartering involves is consistent with potential expanded roles for school councils along the lines just mentioned.[18]

Again, however, the prospects for charter schools in Ontario in the near term are not good. The bulk of the players at the provincial level have either strong vested interest in the current system, or find the ideas of decentralization and local empowerment that inspire charter schools just plain weird. A telling illustration of this unpromising combination occurred when the EIC released its 1997 report on the future of school boards (EIC 1997). Following hearings whose line-ups reflected the financial and organizational power of teacher unions and schools boards, the EIC recommended that Ontario not establish charter schools, a recommendation that was both gratuitous—the EIC's mandate for the investigation had asked no such question—and based on no research.[19]

Expanding Choice with Partial Funding of Independent Schools

If the movement toward more effective school governance in the publicly funded system is stalled, the obvious alternative is to make the advantages of schools that already have autonomous governance—the province's independent schools—available to parents who cannot now afford them. Ontario is the only Canadian province outside the Atlantic region that provides no financial support to independent schools. Neither the federal nor provincial income tax provides relief for elementary- and secondary-school tuition, so even modestly priced independent schools pose a burden that most families, especially those with several children, are ill positioned to bear.

The fact that, despite this burden, independent school enrolment is growing far faster than enrolment in the publicly funded system testifies to the attraction of more autonomous schools. The appeal of many of these schools to families stems partly from the characteristics of other families that choose them, but that is not the whole story. Large-scale research on achievement scores of students from similar social backgrounds testifies to independent schools' ability to do more—and at lower cost—than their public counterparts, and the results appear strongest for minority students in large cities. It is intriguing to note the tendency for jurisdictions whose IALS scores showed a looser link between achievement and socioeconomic status to be those offering more choice.[20] Cause and effect are open to debate, and the sample is small, but this evidence is consistent with the view that choice offers less advantaged families more opportunity to send their kids to better schools. Any increase in the dispersion of achievement caused by better-motivated families moving their kids first is overcome in the longer term by the pressure on inferior schools to improve.[21]

Like charter legislation, formulas for independent school funding are available off the shelf. British Columbia, for example, provides qualifying independent schools with per-student grants equal to either 50 or 35 percent of the adjusted per-student cost of the local public district. The larger grant goes to schools with per-student operating costs equal to or less than those of the local district; the smaller grant to those whose costs are above it.[22] Alberta is currently phasing in a funding formula for independent schools that will provide an amount equal to 60 percent of the per-student basic grant provided to public schools.[23] Alberta's formula is not sensitive to, and places no restriction on, independent school fees or operating costs, although it does require independent schools to operate for one year before becoming eligible for funding. In both provinces, independent schools receiving funds are subject to audit and inspection by the provincial ministry of education.

As this book was going to press, the Ontario government had just presented a budget in which it proposed to establish a tax credit for independent school tuition. Once mature, in five years' time, the tax credit will be worth $3,500. This approach has much the same effect as direct grants to independent schools would have, although there are some important distinctions. On the positive side, the parents continue to pay the entire tuition, rather than facing the dilution of the purchaser/provider relationship that direct grants might create. On the negative side, the packaging of the funding initiative as a tax measure means that the cost will not appear, as it ought to do, as part of the education ministry's budget, which means that achieving savings as students move from the public to the independent system will require more political courage and management acumen.

That said, tax credits for tuition at independent schools that are willing and able to qualify is attractive because they are simpler and quicker to implement than legislation giving school councils (potential) executive powers or allowing the creation of charter schools. They will immediately lower the barriers to families with limited means who wish to withdraw their children from under-performing schools. As long as the departure of those children is reflected through the per-student funding formula to the regular public system, they would provide an immediate spur to under-performing boards and schools to turn themselves around.

As the budget proposal recognized, moreover, the cost of partial funding can be tailored to the provincial budget— low at the start, when it would represent a net addition to current education spending, and more generous later, when growing independent school enrolment began to tip the balance to a net saving (Box 1). There might be indirect savings as well, since the widespread current practice whereby boards fight budgetary restraint by making the most painful cuts first would be harder to sustain when independent schools were operating nearby on lower budgets (OQE 2000, 3). This is an area where good education policy will free up fiscal resources in the long term—money that could be applied to other purposes, even including judicious investments in the fully funded public system.[24]

It is encouraging that polling numbers suggest that funding independent schools is politically viable. When pollsters ask what schools should receive funding, provided they meet provincial standards, a plurality (around 40 percent) support the status quo, about one-quarter favour funding regular public schools only—that is, defunding all Catholic schools—and about one-third support funding for other religious schools also or, more frequently, all private schools (Livingstone et al. 2000). There is already a sizeable constituency for independent-school funding, and principled political leadership should be able to increase its size.

In a diverse, tolerant society such as Ontario, fears of religious fragmentation are easily countered by evidence that achievement and behaviour are, to say the least, no worse in religious schools than in secular ones, and that the graduates of religious schools are every bit as good citizens as graduates of public schools.[25] The argument that independent school funding or tuition tax credits will drain hundreds of millions of dollars from the public system presupposes that current publicly funded schools are so bad that offering alternatives would produce a mass exodus—clearly an argument for offering alternatives. Not only would tens of thousands of students attend better schools, but if the province reduced grants proportionately to the boards they were leaving (as described in Box 1), there would be unprecedented moves to replace poorly performing trustees, bureaucrats, principals, teachers and programs with better ones.[26]

Box 1   Potential Fiscal Impact of Tax Credit for Independent School Tuition

---

The Ontario government has proposed a tax credit for independent-school tuition. The credit, which would be refundable, would offset 10 percent of tuition costs up to a maximum tuition of $7000 for students enrolled in qualifying independent schools in 2002. It would rise by an additional 10 percent annually until it reaches 50 percent—$3,500 for the maximum tuition of $7000—in 2006. How might this credit affect the provincial budget? Making such an estimate requires a number of assumptions.

First, as far as total system costs are concerned, suppose that
- total enrolment in all schools grows 1.4 percent annually from a 2002/03 level of 2.23 million; and
- per-student spending in the publicly funded system grows at 3 percent annually (2 percent inflation plus 1 percent real) from a 2002/03 level of $6,700.

Turning to the independent sector, suppose that
- enrolment would have grown at its historical rate of 3.5 percent from a 2002/03 level of 97,000 without the tax credit;
- the credit causes the share of students attending independent schools to rise by 4 percentage points (not quite to the level in British Columbia) over 5 years, with the increase occurring in equal annual percentage amounts;

	Base Enrolment in Independent Schools 000s	Incremental Enrolment in Independent Schools 000s	Total Enrolment in Independent Schools 000s	Eligible Students 000s
2002	100	0	100	90
2003	104	15	119	107
2004	108	32	140	126
2005	111	54	165	149
2006	115	80	195	176

Note: Numbers may not multiply exactly due to rounding.
Source: Author's calculations as explained in the text.

- delays in certification, and failure or refusal of some schools to participate, means that 90 percent of students at independent schools attend schools that qualify for the credit; and
- half of students attending qualifying schools incur tuition in excess of the $7,000 maximum; for the other half, tuition rises 3 percent annually from a 2002/03 average of $6,000.

The fiscal impact of the tax credit under these assumptions is illustrated in the table. In the first year, the credit is an additional cost to the province, since there is no migration of students from the fully funded to the independent sector. In each subsequent year, however, movement to the independent sector reduces costs in the fully funded sector, offsetting the increase in the value of the credit. By 2006, when phase-in is complete, the saving to the fully funded system equals the cost of the credit.

Potential savings, as students transfer from the fully funded to the independent sector, will not automatically be realized, but will require political determination. In the scenario illustrated here, enrolment in the fully funded system would still grow—the fixed costs would not be spread over a smaller number of students—but savings might be realized as departing students curb the rate of enrolment growth. The more important question is whether or not migration of students from fully-funded to independent schools *ought* to reduce funds to the boards that lose students. In my view, it should: the prod of reduced funding is a key element in the tax credit's potential to induce the fully-funded system to perform better.

Average Tax Credit $	Cost of Tax Credit $ millions	Per-student Grant in Fully Funded System $	Saving to Fully Funded System $ millions	Net Fiscal Impact of Tax Credit $ millions
650	59	6,700	0	59
1,318	141	6,901	101	40
2,005	253	7,108	231	22
2,711	404	7,321	396	8
3,438	604	7,541	604	0

Privately Funded Vouchers

Even with tax credits in place, however, independent school tuition will still impose a barrier to many low-income parents. For that reason, it would also be desirable for private entrepreneurs and philanthropists to establish scholarships that would help even small numbers of students leave poorly performing publicly funded schools for better independent ones. Since other contributors to this volume take the subject of private scholarships up further, I will make only two observations.

First, US experience suggests that such programs, even on a limited scale, spread their benefits beyond the few families able to participate. Like partial funding of independent schools, private vouchers can spur improvements in the schools and boards the students leave, benefitting those who stay as well as those who go.[27] And if US experience is any guide, the actual use of private vouchers by lower-income families will help dispel one of the most pernicious myths propagated by opponents of parental choice: the myth that poor people are unable or unwilling to pick good schools for their children.[28]

Second, private scholarships will be a more powerful tool for inducing change in publicly funded schools than, say, corporate funding for computers in the classroom, or forums in which educational "insiders" and businesspeople vie in emphasizing their commitment to education. Funding and praise are useful motivators, but they are less powerful in keeping an enterprise focused on serving its customers well than fear that ill-served customers will take their business elsewhere.[29]

Concluding Thoughts

To sum up, deadlock seems an apt way to characterize the current state of publicly funded education in Ontario. The centralizing thrust of policy has produced an environment where local schools, those who work in them, and the families whose children attend them, have little influence, and where bottom-up pressure to improve is extraordinarily weak. On their face, the prospects for raising the average achievement of Ontario students and narrowing the large gap between those from more and less promising socioeconomic circumstances do not look good.

Discouraging though this prospect is, promising options lie close to hand. The province's move toward testing represents an important first step in setting standards for achievement and measures of progress. Similarly, per-student funding and the existence of school councils in most Ontario schools are key elements in a system that could create bottom-up pressure to meet those standards. The next step is to empower schools and families so that this bottom-up pressure begins to work.

Ideally, that empowerment would involve two complementary measures. On the governance side, schools would receive new powers over staffing, budget, and program, either through new decision-making authority for principals and councils that wish it, or through charter-school legislation, or both. On the funding side, implementation of the tax credit for independent school tuition, and ensuring that departures from the fully-funded system are reflected in cuts in per-student grants, will create competitive pressures for schools to use their autonomy in the service of student achievement.

This book should make a welcome contribution toward making those alternatives more familiar. And if it inspires the creation of even a small program of private scholarships, it will do two more things. It will provide previously unimagined opportunities to at least a few less well off families. And it will demonstrate how parental choice can generate powerful bottom-up pressure for better schools.

References

Adams, M. J. 1990. *Beginning to Read: Thinking and Learning about Print*. Cambridge, Mass.: MIT Press.

Alberta. 1998. "Government Accepts Private Schools Funding Task Force Recommendations." Alberta Education News Release. (5 March).

American Institutes for Research. 1999. *An Educators' Guide to Schoolwide Reform*. Internet at www.aasa.org/Reform/index.htm.

Angus Reid Group. 1998. "The Public's Esteem for Selected Professions." Toronto. (10 November).

Angus Reid Group. 1999. "Canadians' Assessment and Views of the Education System." Toronto. (22 June).

Angus Reid Group. 2000. "A Failing Grade for Ontario's Public School System." Toronto. (3 March).

Bedard, K., and C. Ferrall. 1997. "Wage and Test Score Dispersion: Some International Evidence," Queen's University working paper.

Betts, J.R. 1996. "Is There a Link between School Inputs and Earnings? Fresh Scrutiny of an Old Literature." In G. Burtless, ed. *Does Money Matter? The Effect of School Resources on Student Achievement and Adult Success*. Washington, DC: The Brookings Institution.

Bishop, John. 1998. "High School Diploma Examinations: Do Students Learn More? Why?" *Policy Options*. July/August.

Bosetti, L., E. Foulkes, R. O'Reilly and Dave Sande. 2000. *Canadian Charter Schools at the Crossroads.* Kelowna: Society for the Advancement of Excellence in Education.

Brennan, Richard. 2000. "No Cash for Religious Schools, Harris Says." *Toronto Star.* (19 January).

British Columbia (BC). 1999. *General Independent Schools Information.* Ministry of Education, Office of the Inspector of Independent Schools. (June).

Canadian Psychological Association (CPA). 1992. *Position Paper on Beginning Reading Instruction.* Ottawa. (June).

Chall, J. S. 1967. *Learning to Read: The Great Debate.* New York: McGraw-Hill.

Coleman, J.S. and T. R. Hoffer. 1987. *Public and Private High Schools.* New York: Basic Books.

Coleman, Peter. 1994. *Learning about Schools: What Parents Need to Know and How They Can Find Out.* Montreal: Institute for Research on Public Policy.

Cornwall, Claudia. 1998. "Scandal of Our Illiterate Kids." *Readers Digest Canada.* (May).

Coulson, Andrew. 1999. *Market Education: The Unknown History.* New Brunswick, N.J.: Transaction Books.

Daly, Rita. 1994. "How Adequate is 'Adequate' in School Literacy Tests?" *Toronto Star.* (5 July).

Education Improvement Commission (EIC). 1997. *A Report on the Roles of School Boards and Trustees.* Toronto.

Education Improvement Commission (EIC). 1998. *A Report on the Role of School Councils.* Toronto.

Education Quality and Accountability Office (EQAO).1998. *Selected Research Highlights TIMMS Population 2 (13-Year-Olds).* Toronto. (April).

Education Quality and Accountability Office (EQAO). 1999. Provincial Report on Achievement: English Language Schools. Toronto.

Education Quality and Accountability Office (EQAO). 2000a. *Ontario Provincial Report on Achievement, 1999-2000.* Toronto.

Education Quality and Accountability Office (EQAO). 2000b. *Parent Handbook, 2000-2001.* Toronto.

Englemann, S., et al. 1988. "The Direct Instruction Follow Through Model: Design and Outcomes." *Education and Treatment of Children* 11 (4).

Finn, Chester E., Jr., Gregg Vanourek, Bruno V. Manno. 2000. *Charter Schools in Action: Renewing Public Education.* Princeton, N.J.: Princeton University Press.

Foorman, B.R., D.J. Francis, J.M. Fletcher, C. Schatschneider, and P. Mehta. 1998. "The Role of Instruction in Learning to Read: Preventing Reading Failure in At-risk Children." *Journal of Educational Psychology,* 90 (115).

Frempong, G. and J. D. Willms. 1999. *Mathematics: The Critical Filter.* Atlantic Centre for Policy Research Policy Brief No. 5. University of New Brunswick. (March).

Hanushek, E. 1996. "School Resources and Student Achievement." In Burtless, G. ed., *Does Money Matter? The Effect of School Resources on Student Achievement and Adult Success.* Washington D.C., The Brookings Institution.

Hill, P. T., G. E. Foster and T. Gendler. 1990. *High Schools with Character.* RAND R-3944-RC.

Holmes, Mark. 1998. *The Reformation of Canada's Schools: Breaking the Barriers to Parental Choice.* Montreal and Kingston: McGill-Queen's University Press.

Hunter, Ian. 2000. "Can The Universities Be Saved?" *National Report.* (24 January).

Kelly, Bernadette F. 1993/94. "Sacrosanctity versus Science: Evidence and Education Reform." *Effective School Practices.* (Fall).

Kuhn, Peter. 1998. "The Declining Labour Market Outcomes of the Less Skilled: Can Fiscal Policy Make a Difference?" *Canadian Public Policy* 24 (3).

Lapointe, Archie E., Janice M. Askew, and Nancy A. Mead. 1992a. *Learning Science.* Princeton, NJ: Educational Testing Service.

Lapointe, Archie E., Nancy A. Mead, and Janice M. Askew. 1992b. *Learning Mathematics.* Princeton, NJ: Educational Testing Service.

Lapointe, Archie E., Nancy A. Mead, and Gary W. Phillips. 1989. *A World of Differences: An International Assessment of Mathematics and Science.* Princeton, NJ: Educational Testing Service.

Lewington, Jennifer, and Graham Orpwood. 1993. *Overdue Assignment: Taking Responsibility for Canada's Schools.* Toronto: John Wiley & Sons Canada.

Lewington, Jennifer. 1994. "Rae's Education Comments Cause Shock." *Globe and Mail* (27 October).

Lindsay, D. 1995. "Pepsico Backs Off Voucher Plan in Jersey City." *Education Week.* (15 November).

Livingstone, D.W., D. Hart and L.E. Davie. 2000. *Public Attitudes toward Education in Ontario, 1998: The Twelfth OISE/UT Survey.* Toronto: Ontario Institute for Studies in Education/University of Toronto.

McLean, L.D., D. Raphael, and M.W. Wahlstrom. 1984. *Intentions and Attainments in the Teaching and Learning of Mathematics: Report on the Second International Mathematics Study.* Toronto: Ontario Institute for Studies in Education.

Maloney, Michael. 1998. *Teach Your Children Well: A Solution to Some of North America's Educational Problems.* Cambridge, Mass.: Cambridge Center for Behavioral Studies.

Morris, Chris. 2000. "High school dumbed-down: Profs say know-nothing grads not ready for university" *The Canadian Press.* (17 February).

Neal, D. 1998. "What Have We Learned about the Benefits of Private Schooling?" *Federal Reserve Bank of New York Economic Policy Review.* Vol. 4, Number 1. (March).

Nolan, Dan. 2000. "Tories Ready to Take it Down a Notch." *Hamilton Spectator.* (14 February).

Ontario, Ministry of Education and Training (MET). 1992a. *Mathematics Grade 8: A Report for Educators.* Toronto: Queen's Printer for Ontario.

———. 1992b. *Mathematics Grade 10 (General Level): A Report for Educators.* Toronto: Queen's Printer for Ontario.

———.1992c. *Mathematics Grade 12 (Advanced Level): A Report for Educators.* Queen's Printer for Ontario.

Ontario Parent Council (OPC). 1998. *Submission to the Education Improvement Commission.* (2 October).

Ontario Progressive Conservative Caucus. 1992. *A Blueprint for Learning in Ontario.* Toronto. (October).

Organization for Quality Education (OQE). 2000. "Financial Support for Qualifying Independent Schools: a Policy Proposal." Waterloo. (3 February).

Robertson, Lesley. 1999. "Clackmannanshire Early Learning Initiative: Third Progress Report." Clackmannanshire Council. (27 October).

Robitaille, D.F. 1998. "How Are Canadian Students Doing?" *Policy Options*. (July-August).

Robitaille, D.F., A.R. Talyor and G. Orpwood. 1997. The TIMSS-Canada Report, Volume One: Grade 8. Vancouver: Department of Curriculum Studies, University of British Columbia.

Robson et al. 1999. *Could Still Do Better*. Toronto: Ontario Coalition for Education Reform.

Statistics Canada and Council of Ministers of Education, Canada (SC/CMEC). 2000. *Education Indicators in Canada Report of the Pan-Canadian Education Indicators Program 1999*. Ottawa. (February).

Schweitzer, Thomas. 1998. "The Third International Mathematics and Science Study: The Achievement of Canada's High School Students Is Fairly Strong." *OQE Forum* 7 (3).

Sweet, L. 1998. *God in the Classroom: The Controversial Issue of Religion in Canada's Schools*. Toronto: McClelland & Stewart.

United States Department of Education (US DOE). 2000. *The State of Charter Schools 2000*. Washington: Office of Educational Research and Improvement. (January).

Watson, Joyce E., and Rhona S. Johnston. 1998. "Accelerating Reading Attainment: The Effectiveness of Synthetic Phonics." University of St. Andrews School of Psychology mimeograph.

Willms, J. D. 1997. *Literacy Skills of Canadian Youth*. Ottawa: Statistics Canada and Human Resource Development Canada, Catalogue 89-552-MPE, No. 1.

Wolfe, Richard, David Wiley and Ross Traub. 1999. *Psychometric Perspectives for EQAO: Generalizability Theory and Applications*. EQAO Research Series Number 3. Toronto: Education Quality and Accountability Office. (August).

Notes

1   In 1995, the last year for which comparative data are available, per student spending in Ontario's elementary and secondary schools was $7,617, nearly 9 percent higher than the next-ranked province of Quebec, and 14 percent above the Canadian average. Converted to US dollars at purchasing-power-parity exchange rates, Ontario's spending was roughly equal to the OECD leader, the United States, and nearly 50 percent higher than the OECD average (SC/CMEC 2000, 212)

2   In the 1982 Second International Mathematics Study and the 1988 and 1991 International Assessments of Educational Progress, Ontario's results, lower than those of other provinces, dragged Canada's overall scores down to middling levels on the international scale (McLean et al., 1984; Lapointe et al., 1989; Lapointe et al., 1992a and 1992b).

3   Ontarians tend to console themselves that at least they outdo their neighbours to the south, but Alberta was the only province to outrank the US average in either subject; Ontario was well below it.

4   TIMSS also tested the final year of high school, with results that were more encouraging but harder to interpret. In the countries covered, nearly all children of elementary and middle-school age are in school and taking most sub-

jects. By school-leaving age, however, this is not so, leading the test designers to focus on the top 10 percent of students in selected countries. In math, Ontario's top students scored relatively well; in science, however, their performance was in the lower half of the rankings. In both cases, the positive nature of these results was muted by the absence of the perennially strong performing Asian countries (Robitaille 1998), and by the fact that most Ontario students had received 13 years of schooling, rather than the 11 or 12 typical elsewhere (Schweitzer 1998, 8).

5 A summary of SAIP results can be found in SC/CMEC 1999, 78-79, 223-24.

6 Provinces with appreciable bilingual populations report for anglophone and francophone students separately.

7 An early striking study of the dispersion in marks assigned in such tests is Diederich, French, and Carlton 1961. Wolfe, Riley and Traub (1999) estimate that the accuracy rates of individual marks in the 1997 EQAO tests was between 70 and 80 percent. These authors claim that such accuracy is similar to that found in multiple-choice tests, but multiple-choice tests have no marking errors of this type: the performance-based tests add a further layer of uncertainty to problems such as inexact match with curriculum and variations in individual performance at different times that are common to both types of tests.

8 These are shares of the entire population, including students who were exempted or submitted work that was judged impossible to score. The introduction of a new curriculum complicates comparisons between elementary-level results in 1997 and those in later years.

9 The proportions had not changed in problem-solving and geometry. EQAO 1997.

10 Panel b of Table 2, which shows absolute numbers, might appear unduly hard on boards with large student populations. From the perspective of an evaluator or policymaker seeking to reduce the number of students missed by these tests, however, it might make sense to focus more on reducing the rates in relatively large boards.

11 Principals have the power to exempt students from the EQAO tests "if a student would be unable to participate productively or if her or his participation would be harmful" (EQAO 2000b, 20).

12 Enrolment figures are available under "Quick Facts" at www.edu.gov.on.ca.

13 Since many homeschoolers do not register their children, it is hard to be sure about the true number. The fact that the two leading home-schooling organizations in Ontario have 2,000 families as members, many with more than one child at home, suggests a likely total of around 5,000.

14 Project Follow-Through researchers graded nine education approaches according to their effectiveness in raising students' scores in basics, cognitive concepts, and affective outcomes such as sense of self-worth. Direct instruction dominated other approaches, not only for basic knowledge and problem-solving skills, but for raising students' self-esteem. The study has received far more attention among outsiders to the education system than it has among insiders (Kelly 1993/94); among Canadian teachers, it seems to be virtually unknown (Maloney 1998, 184).

15   In the 1997 SAIP, for example, 71 percent of 16-year-olds in full-year programs
       scored at or above the expected levels in math, compared to 55 percent of their
       semestered counterparts.

16   Research into the relationship—or, more accurately, lack of it (Hanushek 1996)—
       between money spent and student achievement has tentatively identified
       bureaucratization and centralization as explanations for the failure of more
       money to improve schools over the last generation (Betts 1996).

17   In the 1997/98 school year, the share of white students attending US charter
       schools was more than 10 percentage points below the share of white students
       attending regular public schools in chartering states, with higher enrolments
       among blacks, Hispanics and students of aboriginal origin making up the differ-
       ence. Charter schools enrolled a higher proportion of students eligible for lunch
       subsidies than did other schools in chartering states (US DOE 2000, 30, 34).

18   About one-fifth of US charter schools are converted regular public schools, ten
       percent are converted private schools; the rest are start-ups. Of those that had
       been regular public schools, more than one third who responded to a Depart-
       ment of Education survey said they switched to gain autonomy and flexibility
       (US DOE 2000, 14, 43).

19   The EIC report's bibliography contained not one reference to the voluminous
       US literature on charter schools, nor to any Canadian writings on the subject.
       An EIC staffer confirmed to me that there was no research to support this
       recommendation.

20   The four Canadian provinces with relatively flat gradients have all provided
       funding to at least some independent schools for many years. Among the coun-
       tries, Sweden and the Netherlands, which have well established independent
       school funding, had much flatter gradients than the United States, Britain, and
       New Zealand, where such schemes do not exist or are relatively new (Frempong
       and Willms, 1999, 2).

21   See the chapter by Caroline Hoxby in this volume for further evidence of the
       benefits of choice among public schools on student achievement and efficiency.

22   The adjustment subtracts funds related to capital items as well as several special-
       education categories. A brief summary of independent school funding and regu-
       lation in British Columbia can be found in BC 1999.

23   Independent schools in Alberta receive no funds for transportation, capital, or
       maintenance, and have no access to education property taxes. A special regime
       covers special-education students. A quick brief summary of recent changes in
       independent school funding in Alberta can be found in Alberta 1998.

24   British Columbia's Office of the Inspector of Independent Schools estimates
       that educating the province's independent school students in the public system
       would add more than $130 million in annual operating grants to the provincial
       education budget, and impose a further $750-million to $1 billion in new capi-
       tal funding (BC 1999).

25   For an account from a *Toronto Star* reporter who took a year studying religious
       schools and emerged with her initial negative prejudices undone, see Sweet
       1998. See also the chapter by Jay Greene in this volume, where he compares the
       effect of public and private schools on the civic values of their students and
       graduates.

26 For a number of accounts of such turnarounds, see Finn et al. 2000.

27 Again, whether this potential is realized depends partly on the provincial government's willingness to ensure that lower enrollment is reflected in proportionately lower funding.

28 For a useful account of evidence about the primacy of academic concerns and the desire for more discipline in the classroom among lower-income US families with children in independent schools, see Coulson (1999, 260-62).

29 The experience of Pepsi, which announced that it would donate to a voucher program for low-income children in Jersey City, provides a cautionary tale. The company withdrew the offer in the face of boycott threats by the public-school teachers union and widespread attacks on their vending machines (Lindsay 1995). Foundations and other organizations less exposed to intimidation may be better placed to see such programs through.

Reinventing Public Education Via the Marketplace

Chester E. Finn, Jr.

Usually I'm known as a Cassandra, full of bad news, or as an extremist wanting to do horrible things. But after reading some of the other papers in this book I feel like an optimist and a moderate. I bring you news of energy, activity, and good things happening south of the border, more and better things than I have seen in twenty-five years in the education field. Unlike Andrew Coulson and others who think that the government ought to dry up and blow away, I come to discuss the reinvention rather than the obliteration of public education. Like a number of contributors, I bring a US perspective to this Canadian discussion, and my purpose is to outline a few education reform ideas underway in the United States and their prospects for reinventing the system.

Solution 1: More Funding for Public Schools

When it comes to repairing our public education systems there are three major ideas circulating in the United States. The first is not a very big

This paper is an edited version of the keynote speech Chester E. Finn, Jr. made at the Fraser Institute conference, *School Choice: Dispelling the Myths and Examining the Evidence*, April 1, 2000.

idea; it is rather a familiar, old idea. You could call it more of the same: fix the schools with more input—smaller classes, more teachers, more teacher training, more technology, more special programs, more hours in the day, more days in the year, et cetera. In both Canada and the United States, this has long been our chief approach to making schools better. It is like our chief approach to making lots of things better: install a larger engine, replace the tires, and add more chrome. In pursuit of this strategy, per pupil spending in the United States has tripled in real terms since the 1950s.

The main problem with this strategy is that it has not worked. It has not worked if by working we mean significantly boosting student achievement. Scores remain essentially flat, reflecting an unacceptably low level of student performance. In international comparisons of advanced nations, American students are in the basement by the end of high school. They did pretty well in the fourth grade and middling in eighth grade, leading some observers to remark that the United States is the only major country in the world where the longer kids stay in school the dumber they get.

Solution 2: Standards and Incentives

The strategy of ever-increasing inputs, used for most of the past decade, has failed. Many of our states have now embarked upon a second approach to education reform. Some call it standards-based reform or systemic reform. It starts with the premise that if we care most about academic results, we need to focus directly on those results. The way to begin is to specify the results we want. As Alice in Wonderland was told, spell out clearly the destination for your journey and you have a chance of getting there. This strategy includes installing reliable measures of progress in relation to the standards and tests, and then making schools accountable for their results. That is, we should reward teachers and administrators when they achieve the desired results and intervene in some way when they don't. This approach might mean extra pay for teachers and principals whose students meet the standards. It might mean summer school for the child who does not meet the standards. And if lots of his classmates are also not meeting the standards, it might mean a loss of job security for the grown-ups working in that school.

The complexities of standards-based reform make it difficult to implement. Who sets the standards? After an aborted effort at national standards in the US we have pretty much settled on state standards. Do the tests accurately reflect the standards? Are they valid and informative? Hardest of all, do policy-makers have the fortitude to enforce accountability even when it turns out that a very large number of children are not meeting the standards? If a large number of the schools or school systems in the state turn out not to meet the standards, it may get a little awkward for the politicians in charge. If the majority of the people in your state fail to meet your state's standard and you want to get re-elected, it gets difficult to remain rigorous about enforcement.

Solution 3: Market-based Approaches

Between the "do more" strategy and the "standards-based" strategy, a third education reform strategy has started to take hold. It is the strategy that today's conference is mostly about. This one avoids centralized, top-down change. It reflects grassroots, marketplace, competition-style change. For simplicity, we often call it the choice movement, though it takes many forms. The choice movement includes vouchers, charter schools, contract or out-sourced schools, all sorts of privately funded scholarship programs, open enrolment plans, public-school choice plans and other ways to foster diversity and competition in primary and secondary education. The theory behind it, which I subscribe to, holds that the regular system is most likely to change in response to pressure from competition. In many states, the standards-based reform paradigm is trying to co-exist with the marketplace reform paradigm. Sometimes they collide; usually they complement one another. Unfortunately, people tend to believe, as a matter of faith or doctrine, in one or the other: most people believe either in standards-based reform or in marketplace-based reform. I have come to believe in both.

Charter Schools

The reinvention of public education is the foremost goal of the marketplace reform paradigm. I am going to illustrate this with the charter school example and then say a brief word about four other forms of school choice that are also part of marketplace reform. I'm not going to say much about vouchers because they are well covered by other contributors to this book.

Charter schools are independent public schools free from most of the bureaucratic constraints of state and local regulations and in most places free from teacher-union contract provisions. They can be conversions of existing public schools. In some states, they can be conversions of existing private schools. Most, though, are brand new schools started by teachers, parents, community groups, and even private firms.

Charter schools are spreading rapidly in the United States. We have 2000 of them today, enrolling 500,000 children. Clinton's education secretary, Richard Riley, predicted that there will be 3000 of them by 2002, and said that he welcomes this prospect. This has been a bi-partisan movement, and both the 2000 presidential candidates sought more charter schools as part of their education programs.[1]

The charter school movement began in 1992 when the first US charter school opened its doors in Minnesota. Today about 15 percent of all the children in the District of Columbia attend 31 charter schools. About 15 percent of the children in Kansas City also attend charter schools, which have been in existence for only two years in that city. In the state of Arizona, which has the liveliest charter school movement in the country, charter schools now comprise one-fifth of all the schools in the state, enrolling some seven percent of all children.

Roughly 70 percent of all charter schools are brand new schools; about 19 percent are pre-existing public schools that converted, and 11 percent are pre-existing private schools that converted. By converting to charter schools, those private schools give up their private status and any religious affiliation.

Charter schools are indisputably a form of public school, but they are a different kind of public school than we are accustomed to. Traditionally in the US, as I think in Canada, we have equated public schools with government-run schools. If you asked anyone, "What's the definition of a public school?" you would be told, "a school run by a school system run by the government." Charter schools don't fit that definition. They are not run by a bureaucracy, but they are still public schools in three very important ways.

First, charter schools are open to everyone. They do not have admission standards. They must accept all children they have room to take. Second, charter schools are paid for with tax dollars; they do not charge tuition. And third, charter schools are accountable to a duly constituted public authority for their results, which is to say that they can be shut down if their results are unsatisfactory. A charter school has a specific time period, typically five years, to deliver the results it promised, and if it doesn't deliver those results, it risks not having its charter renewed.

At the same time, because it is a school of choice, a charter school must satisfy its clients or it will find itself without students. In other words, a charter school is accountable in two directions, to the public body that authorized it and also to the families that enrol their children in it. That's why about 80 charter schools, 4 percent of them, have already closed or shut down. Failed charter schools close. How many failed public schools can we say that about?

Because charter schools remain public schools they do not satisfy school choice purists, and they do not satisfy single-minded market partisans. Though they are more independent than traditional public schools and though they are attended only by youngsters whose families select them, they are in fact still overseen by government, are vulnerable to shifts in the political winds, and are subject to an imperfect marketplace. Yet they are not conventional public schools, either. That's why the public school establishment looks askance at them. They aren't subject to all of the public school regulations and union contract provisions, and they don't have to hire certified teachers. They are more apt to be run by lay people than by experts, and they signal to the nation that, far from being guaranteed pupils and budgets, they must satisfy their customers and live up to their obligations.

Because charter schools are neither fish nor fowl, we probably ought not to expect either market purists or the public education establishment to embrace them. That may, however, also be their genius, the source of their broad political appeal and the basis for much of their popular appeal. As we can see, they are already having an impact. Imagine a 10 or 15 percent market shift in just two or three years for any new product! And then consider how new charter schools are. The average one is less than three years old which means that a lot of families must be desperate: they are taking a chance on brand new schools with no track records, meager funding, often housed in makeshift facilities.

Funding formulas for these schools are often complicated, but they typically don't get capital funding from the state and usually average about 80 percent of what regular public schools get by way of operating dollars. How desperate do you have to be to take your own child into something as risky as that? Yet as of 2001, they enrol half a million children, and 70 percent of all US charter schools have waiting lists. The demand for them exceeds the supply.

My colleagues and I recently published a book called *Charter Schools in Action*. In it, we explore what an "all-charter" future might look like. One of the chapters takes an imaginary tour through an imaginary large city ten years from now, a city in which all the public schools are charter schools. When we wrote it, we thought that this was fiction, but since then we have seen the numbers starting to swell—those 15 percent enrolment numbers are certainly heading towards twenty and twenty-five percent. Serious people, often from the left, have begun to suggest that all-charters might be the solution to the crisis of urban education in America. The head of the National Urban League has suggested an all-charter arrangement for urban education in America. A mainstream group called the Education Commission of the States has suggested an all-charter school scenario for the governance of public education. We may still be fantasizing, but one day some US community is going to make all its public schools charter schools, and we will be able to see how it works.

Strange things sometimes happen in education reform. We never thought that cities would experiment with vouchers but, lo and behold, we now have several places trying them. We never thought we would see the New York State legislature pass a charter law but, lo and behold, there are now charter schools in New York state, the Kremlin of teacher-union political influence! (It turned out that New York State legislators care about one thing more than they care about the teachers' union: their own pay. When the governor said that under no circumstance would he sign the recent pay raise without first approving the charter school bill, the charter school bill passed! It passed in the state that I thought would be last to pass a charter school law!)

The benefits of charter schools, and other forms of school choice, are apparent in two ways. One benefit applies directly to the youngsters who can go from bad schools to better schools, from dangerous schools to safer schools, and from schools that never teach them to read to schools that teach everybody to read. That's one benefit. The other benefit is that competition turns out to be good for the system, too, even though the system doesn't appreciate it.

In the presence of competition, the system must face the fact that it no longer enjoys a monopoly. If schools want students and the dollars that accompany them, they must attract those students, and in order to attract them they have to provide quality education. Our research suggests that the typical public school reaction to charter schools and school choice passes through four predictable stages.

In stage one, public school boards seek to kill the idea. "Stop it, say no to charter schools," they say. "We will have nothing to do with them."

When stage one fails and the public school establishment recognizes that charter schools are inevitable, their stage two reaction appears. They try to minimize them, to keep charter schools as few, as weak and as regulated as possible. They rationalize that since they can't stop charters cold they must at least prevent them from spreading. Today most of the United States is caught in stage one or two.

The stage three reaction of public schools is to start to compete against those upstart charters. To get kids back, the old public schools start offering what people want. If parents prefer a Montessori school, the public schools ask, why can't we offer that? If it is after-school programs they want, why can't the school system provide that? They want uniforms, why can't the school system offer schools with uniforms. Compete back.

We now have a lot of communities beginning to deal with the competition from charter schools by competing better. They hate it but it's good for them and even more importantly, it's good for the kids attending the system who now must be competed for instead of being taken for granted.

Finally comes stage four, which only a few communities have reached so far. Stage four occurs when public school districts take the charter opportunity and turn it into something that benefits the system. It happens when districts use the charter law to accomplish things not possible under the regular regulations and union contracts. They might start a different kind of school, or staff it differently, or use it as an R and D centre, or use it for youngsters who do not fit into the regular system. A number of communities have begun to use the charter opportunity to their advantage, finding new freedom from both state regulations and union constraints.

Most of the country remains stuck in stages one or two. But we are beginning to see enough examples of stages three and four to prove the theory works. Competition works. It changes systems that were once monopolies. They hate it but they do begin to respond.

I have been pummelling the unions a wee bit here but let me say, because it is a matter of real significance, that by almost everybody's account the first American proponent of charter schools was the late Albert Shanker, the American Federation of Teachers' very distinguished and long-time president. In a 1988 speech at the National Press Club, Shanker spoke about an arrangement that would, in his words,

> enable a school, or any group of teachers within a school, to develop a proposal for how they could better educate youngsters and

then give them a charter to implement that proposal. All of this would be voluntary; no teacher would have to participate and parents would choose whether or not to send their children to a charter school. For its part, the school district would have to agree that as long as teachers continue to want to teach in the charter school and parents continue to send their children there, and there was no precipitant decline in student achievement indicators; it would maintain the school for at least five to ten years.

Al had come back from observing some schools in Germany that inspired him, and he was suggesting that the US do something similar.

How are we doing with these charter schools that Shanker envisioned? The movement is too young for us to have sufficient academic achievement results, so let's be candid. We don't know yet. The typical charter school is 2.8 years old and most of the achievement data available today are state-specific and somewhat mixed. Clients, however, are very happy with what they are getting. All sorts of surveys indicate a very high satisfaction level among both charter parents and students.

Just as importantly, there is a very high satisfaction level among charter-school teachers. This is true not just when teachers are surveyed by people who think charters are a good idea, but also when the National Education Association itself surveys them. The NEA has also found, to its amazement, that teachers like charter schools. They like teaching in them and would like more opportunities to teach in them.

I could go on at greater length about accountability for charter schools, which deserves a whole chapter of its own, but I want to return to the larger idea, which is chartering as part of a reinvented public education system. In this reinvented system, officials play a strategic role, not necessarily a functional role operating the schools themselves. We need to reinvent public education so it is no longer run like the highway department, but instead functions through a wide variety of providers of educational services. Public support of schooling without government provision of schools is probably the simplest way to put it. Or call it fostering decentralized control, entrepreneurial management and grassroots initiative.

The charter movement has brought this possibility to life and, I think, done so more effectively than any other form of school choice today in the United States. But let me briefly mention the four other forms of school choice that I think are most interesting.

Vouchers

First are vouchers. We once thought vouchers would never happen with public funds yet now there are three prominent places in the United States where government money pays for vouchers. More places will soon offer vouchers and, depending on a US Supreme Court ruling on a First Amendment issue, lots more places will offer them the day after tomorrow. But vouchers are not spreading quickly compared to charter schools.

Privately funded vouchers, also known as scholarship programs, *are* spreading quickly. They are cropping up like mushrooms thanks to generous private donors who want to improve the educational opportunities of low-income children. A foundation I am involved in, for example, has helped create one of these programs in Dayton, Ohio. This small community of twenty-two thousand kids has all the problems of a big urban education system but now, with the help of a privately funded scholarship program, about a thousand low-income kids are attending independent and parochial schools. Early results suggest that with the help of these privately funded vouchers, these children are learning more in their new schools than their counterparts in the old schools.

Outsourcing

The second of these four other, marketplace style reforms is outsourcing. Outsourcing is the term used when private operators contract with public school systems to run certain public schools. I spent a couple of years with the Edison Project, one of the two dozen private firms that now undertake these contracts. The Edison Project operated more than 100 public schools in 2000-01. Some of them are charter schools but most of them are operating under contract to public school districts, which have decided to outsource the schools they can't seem to fix. Let's see if someone else can make a difference. The state of Maryland recently contracted with Edison to operate several of the worst schools in Baltimore, schools that have proven unfixable over the last couple of decades. A similar arrangement is underway in Chester-Upland, Pennsylvania. The small town of Inkster, Michigan has contracted with Edison to operate its entire school system.

Home Schooling

The third of these four market-style reforms is home schooling. About a million children in the US, about 2 percent of all children, are currently being home-schooled. Their parents have withdrawn from conventional education in favour of teaching their own children at home. There are more of these parents all the time and there are more resources available to them, which leads me to my fourth example because it integrates very nicely with the home schooling example.

Technology

My fourth example is technology. Technology promises to liberate people from physical schools altogether and to enable them to obtain education for their children without ever putting them under the roof of a school building. In a similar way, we have been liberated from travel agents, and our ability to get medical opinion over the Internet has liberated us from doctors. I know several Internet startups that intend to offer a complete elementary/secondary education over the Internet backed by world-class curriculum and instruction, and they intend to market it directly to parents. We already have two dozen virtual schools in the United States. Some of them are charter schools. The first virtual charter school in Ohio was established recently and California already has a half dozen of them.

I used to be something of a Luddite, but now I think we are going discover that children can be educated anywhere: at a school, at home, at the YMCA, or at a parent's workplace, in the study room that will be created there. Using a wide variety of sources of curriculum and instruction—some of which will come through the computer, some through the mail, some in the form of a CD-ROM, and some as videotapes or audiocassettes—parents will choose to combine different forms of instruction. If they don't want their children to be educated in only one place, they will send them to school for the morning and somewhere else for the afternoon. Other parents will supplement their child's education after school. Our one million home scholars could easily become several million if parents no longer had to think up the curriculum and the pedagogy themselves, once it became readily available to them from third party sources. I know this is going to happen because I know people who intend to make it happen, who have lots of money with which to make it inevitable. Like the Internet, virtual schooling is bound to have worldwide consequences. If you can sit in Idaho or Ohio and take advantage of it, there is no reason that you can not sit in Lucknow or Singapore or even Toronto and access the same opportunities for your children.

I have said enough to suggest why I am optimistic for the first time in a quarter of a century in this field. It is not that we have the problems of public education solved, or that any of these reforms is a panacea, a pill that can be swallowed to cure everything tomorrow. No, but the number of remedies, the number of experiments, the number of things that are genuinely different and better is, I think, extremely encouraging. They give us the first outline of how education systems in the United States, Canada, and around the world might be reinvented for the benefit of children, teachers, and the larger society.

Note

1   This speech was given on April 1st, 2000, many months before the election of George W. Bush.

Market Education
and the Public Good

ANDREW J. COULSON,
Senior Fellow, The Mackinac Center,
and Editor, www.SchoolChoices.org

From Canada and the United States to England and Australia, a debate is raging over school governance. The central issue is whether educational systems designed around free market principles and directed by the decisions of families would be superior to the government-run school systems most nations have today. Amidst the great variety of arguments that has been made on both sides of the issue, a general pattern has emerged. Supporters of market education tend to assert that their proposals would increase responsiveness to families and raise academic achievement, while critics argue that market systems could not produce the social benefits we have come to expect from public schooling.

With only a few exceptions, the participants in this debate are talking past one another. Many defenders of public schools acknowledge that there is at least a good chance of achievement improving under a vigorously competitive market, and most admit that competition and parental choice would force schools to cater more closely to the demands of the families they serve. Indeed, some public school supporters oppose market reforms precisely *because* they would cater to the diverse demands of parents. They fear that if parents were completely free to decide the course of their children's education, our societies would be factionalized and balkanized, destroying social cohesion and precipitating conflicts between different ethnic and religious groups.

Based on this assessment, it seems as though the best way out of the muddy rut into which the school choice debate has fallen is to take a hard look at the indirect social effects of market systems and compare them to those of state schooling. If markets prove to be as good or better at producing positive social outcomes, then the debate could take a great leap forward. But even suggesting such a possibility may be too much for some public schooling proponents to stomach. After all, they may be thinking, the very reason public schools were introduced in the first place was to bring literacy and learning to the masses, to promote understanding of and participation in democratic life, to ensure that all children had access to a good education regardless of family income, and to promote social cohesion. Given these raisons d'être, how could public schools *not* be superior to market systems in creating social goods?

Such a view is entirely understandable given the aforementioned conception of the origins of public schooling. If we want people to seriously address the question of social outcomes under market versus state schooling, we first need to show that it is even worth asking. One way to do that is to have a brief look at the history of Canada's public schools, to see whether or not it bears out our assumptions.

How Canada Got Its State Schools

The idea that public schooling arose in response to grass-roots public demand, or even that it was a top-down effort to serve the needs of citizens, finds little support in the historical record. As in the vast majority of nations, public schooling was put in place in Canada thanks to the relentless urgings of government-appointed, paternalistic ideologues. The undisputed leader among Canadian promulgators of state schooling was Egerton Ryerson.

Ryerson became assistant superintendent of schools for Upper Canada (now the province of Ontario) in 1844 and was promoted to superintendent two years later. He held the office for three decades and in that time did more to advance the government take-over of education than any other Canadian. Most of his ideas on tax funding and government operation of schools, compulsory attendance, training and regulation of teachers, and even textbook selection and censorship were passed into law during his tenure.

The motivation behind Ryerson's flurry of activity was his profound belief that his fellow citizens, like so many errant sheep, were incapable of looking after themselves and needed to be herded and watched over by a vigilant government. In 1858, he wrote:

> The State, therefore, so far from having nothing to do with the children, constitutes their collective parent, and is bound to ... secure them all that will qualify them to become useful citizens *to* the state (Prentice 1988, 170; emphasis added)

Note that he did not say "useful citizens *of* the state," but rather "useful citizens *to* the state." Ryerson saw himself not as a public servant, bound to ascertain and meet the avowed demands of the people, but as a philosopher king charged with shaping public attitudes along whatever lines he considered best. His contemporary, John Carroll, wrote that Ryerson's ambition had lain "in the direction of influencing public opinion on those questions and measures the carrying of which he deemed to be for the good of the church and the country" (McDonald 1978, 84). Ryerson admitted as much himself, stating that one of his chief occupations was to

> Prepare publications calculated *to teach the people* at large *to appreciate* ... the institutions established amongst them; and to furnish, from time to time, such expositions of great principles and measures *of the administration* as would *secure the proper appreciation and support* of them on the part *of the people* at large. (McDonald 1978, 85; emphasis added)

Rather than trying to make the state serve the will of the people, Ryerson aimed to convince the people to follow the will of the state. "Government operates on mind," he wrote with Orwellian fervour, as "a minister of God" showering its blessings on its subjects (Prentice 1978, 132). Ryerson's nozzle of choice for producing that shower was a centrally planned government education system. Writing to the British Governor of Upper Canada, Ryerson explained that "the youthful mind of Canada," must be "instructed and moulded in the way I have had the honour of stating to your Excellency, if this country is long to remain an appendage to the British Crown" (McDonald 1978, 84).

While studying the educational systems of Europe, Ryerson was greatly inspired by the extent of the royalty's power to manipulate schools in its efforts to produce a docile and supportive citizenry. According to education historian Neil McDonald, Ryerson concluded that the French king ruled with more absolute power than his English counterpart and that this was only possible thanks to total government control "of the French system of education, from the university down to the primary school" (McDonald 1978, 89). Ryerson's confidence in the ability of the French monarchy to use its power effectively was exaggerated, given that the royalists were ousted from power repeatedly during the 19th century, but it is useful to know where his sympathies lay. Thoughts of monarchical power over education clearly gave him much cheer, and he happily concluded that

> democracy, popular opinion to the contrary, was on the wane in Europe and constitutional monarchy was in the ascendancy (McDonald 1978, 89).

Do Canada's Public Schools Deliver the Goods?

The roots of Canadian public schooling thus extend into an unpleasant-smelling pile of autocratic compost rather than into the earthy loam of democracy so often supposed. Still, just because state schooling in Canada was designed and implemented by an anti-democratic monarchist does not mean that the institution is necessarily bad at producing social goods. We should judge it based on its results rather than strictly by its provenance. Our historical reality check has thus served its purpose. Shocked out of our complacency, we are now ready to evaluate public schooling based on how well it actually fulfils our social goals.

So, how are we doing? Canada is certainly suffering less internal turmoil than many other nations, and while its economy is perhaps not the most vigorous in the world, it is at least functioning moderately well. The problem with these kinds of general observations, though, is that it is difficult to decide how much to attribute them to the public schools and how much to other influences such as demographics, civil society, economic policy, etc.

Fortunately, there are some specific cases of social effects that can be clearly traced to government schools. Unfortunately, those effects tend to be negative. Consider government schooling's effects on religious harmony. In deference to a strong Catholic minority, the Constitution

Act of 1867 required the province of Ontario to pay for a separate Catholic school system in addition to the regular public schools. Government funding of Catholic schools continues to this day, while no other religion in the province enjoys such subsidies.

This strikes many Ontarians as unfair, and it drove some parents to appeal to the United Nations Commission on Human Rights. Arieh Waldman filed a complaint with the UN stating that he was forced to pay for his sons' Jewish education while taxpayers subsidized the schooling of Roman Catholic children. In a November 1999 ruling, the United Nations found in Waldman's favour, ruling Ontario's education funding system discriminatory and calling on the federal government to address the problem within 90 days. The ruling had no force of law, but it put Canada in an awkward position—the federal government, after all, had freely chosen to sign the UN Covenant on Human Rights of which Ontario was found to be in violation.

Ottawa's response to the UN was to ask Ontario to comply with the Covenant by extending government funding to all the province's religious schools. Ontario's Premier immediately replied that his government had no intention of complying with the ruling or of altering its funding system in any way. Janet Ecker, the province's Minister of Education, defended Ontario's stand, stating that

> We've been very clear that our goal is a good quality public education system, and the estimates of $300 million needed to fund religious schools would be $300 million that would come out of the public school system. (Brown 2000, On the Web at: http://www. campuslife.utoronto.ca/groups/jsu/news/thestar2.htm)

Ontario's refusal to revise its education funding system has angered families who feel that the province is actively discriminating against them on religious grounds. Given their frustration, one might expect these parents to take the province to court, since Canada's own Charter of Rights and Freedoms (adopted in 1982) also guarantees equal treatment of its citizens regardless of their religion. Section 15, paragraph 1 of the Charter reads as follows (emphasis added):

> *Every individual* is equal before and under the law and *has the right to the* equal protection and *equal benefit of the law* without discrimination and, in particular, without discrimination based on race, national or ethnic origin, colour, *religion* ...

As it happens, a very similar case was already taken to court. In *Adler v. Ontario* ([1996] 3 S.C.R. 609), Canada's Supreme Court ruled that the Charter of Rights and Freedoms was superseded by the Constitution Act of 1867, and upheld Ontario's education funding system. (This will no doubt prove confusing to US readers accustomed to the more binding guarantees offered by the Bill of Rights. It is par for the course in Canada, however, where any provincial government can also veto the national Charter of Rights and Freedoms at its leisure by invoking the so-called "notwithstanding clause.")

Constitutions can be amended, however, and yet, four years after the *Adler* ruling, and more than a year after the UN verdict, the majority of Ontarians seem content to leave the Constitution Act of 1867 untouched, thereby continuing to discriminate against religious minorities. In the words of York University law professor Anne Bayefsky, this will undoubtedly lead to continued "discord and unhappiness and intolerance" (Blackwell 1999). Ontario's public schools, so often defended on the grounds that they are necessary to prevent social discord, are in this case actually creating it.

The province of Quebec also had a religiously-based government school system enshrined by the Constitution Act, but, unlike Ontario, it *has* chosen to abandon that system. On the first of July, 1998, Quebec officially replaced its pair of religious government school systems (Catholic and Protestant) with a pair of linguistic ones (French and English). Under the new system, schools can still offer Protestant or Catholic religious instruction, but it must be optional and students must also have the choice of a secular class in morals and mores (Vu 1998).

The vestiges of devotional religious training in government schools are likely to be short-lived. A 1999 report by a government-appointed task-force recommends the complete secularization of Quebec's public schools. The task-force, headed by Université de Montréal professor Jean-Pierre Proulx, recommends that religion be studied solely for its historical and cultural significance, in an academic, non-devotional fashion (Arnold 1999, Read Online at http://www.cjnews.com/pastissues/99/may6-99/front3.htm).

Has this move toward secular state schooling eliminated the sort of religious conflict caused by Ontario's selective funding of Catholic schools? For some groups, the secularization of state schooling is long overdue. Quebec's largest teachers' union, the Centrale de l'Enseignement du Quebec (CEQ), has joined a coalition advocating complete secularization, stating that "Schools are not churches, they're not temples, they're not mosques, they're schools (Vu 1998)." As the Proulx report declares:

> Parents who want their children to attend schools that reflect their values should look to the private school system. (Arnold 1999, Read online at http://www.cjnews.com/pastissues/99/may6-99/front3.htm)

M. Proulx notwithstanding, some religious parents object to the idea that they would be forced to pay taxes for schools that do not reflect their values and beliefs. The English Speaking Catholic Council (ESCC), for example, has formed its own coalition "to counter the position taken" by the CEQ's coalition (Walker 1998. Read online at: http://www.qfa.qc.ca/escc/98-99AR.htm). In other words, the proposed secularization of government schooling in Quebec is driving the people to organize themselves into separate factions in order to more effectively impose their views on their fellow citizens. It is surely not lost on the reader that this is *exactly* the kind of balkanization that supporters of secularization claim public schools *avoid*.

Alan Borovoy, of the Canadian Civil Liberties Association, has stated that public schools are "one of the main instruments for promoting inter-group co-operation and respect in our communities" (Blackwell 1999). It is hard to reconcile such beliefs with the real conflicts playing out in Quebec and Ontario.

Perhaps, one might argue, these sorts of social conflicts are aberrations and are not inherent in the make-up of government schooling. Or perhaps the issue of religion is unusual and the overall social effects of state schooling are actually positive. Furthermore, even if public schooling does precipitate some social discord, it may still be superior to education markets in its overall social effects. These suggestions are investigated below, in an accelerated roller-coaster ride through the history of education.

A Note on the Uses and Abuses of History

The wary reader, before agreeing to be strapped into this particular roller-coaster, may be concerned about the way in which the historical evidence will be selected and used. History is big, and a motivated researcher can usually find a precedent or two to support almost any argument. Even well-meaning scholars sometimes reach faulty conclusions due to the lack of a reliable method for farming the vast wheat fields of the past.

To minimize such problems in my own research, I have defined the scope of my investigation as the entire span of formal education from ancient times to the present, and I have adopted a careful strategy for comparing the relative merits of alternative school systems. That strategy is comprised of the following three components:

- Observe how similar school systems operate across many different cultural, technological, and economic settings.
- Observe how different school systems operate in similar settings.
- Observe changes in outcomes that occur as a particular society moves from one educational system to another.

The most common error in the use of historical evidence is to select one commendable culture or practice and then suggest it as a model for contemporary policy. The problem, of course, is that what works in one time or place may not work in another. With respect to schooling in particular, there are many factors beyond the classroom walls that affect educational outcomes. The advantage of the strategy I have outlined is that it turns the great variations between cultures into an advantage. Any education system that has consistently produced good (or bad) results across many different settings and time periods may have something very important to teach us.

While this strategy can increase our confidence in generalizations drawn from the historical record, it should not be confused with scientific proof. The past offers no randomly selected control groups or controlled experimental conditions. Readers must use their own judgement in weighing the evidence.

These caveats in place, we can begin our ride. As already noted, this discussion is of necessity highly abridged. Those wanting a more complete treatment can refer to my book *Market Education: The Unknown History*.

The Goods, the Bads and the Uglies

The Social Effects of Schooling across Time and around the World

Mass education has a much longer history than is generally assumed. As far back as the 5th century BCE, schooling among the Greeks began to spread beyond a tiny elite and eventually reached the majority of citizens. The ancient Greek educational experience was far from uniform. In fact, two very different approaches to schooling arose in the city-states of Athens and Sparta, making this an excellent starting point for our historical journey.[1]

Classical Athens was at once the most liberal society of its time and one of the most cohesive. Though it was plagued by some of the same social blights that have afflicted modern nations, such as slavery and sexism, the level of freedom enjoyed by its citizens would not be exceeded for the next two-thousand years. This freedom extended to education, permitting families complete discretion over their children's schooling. Government played no role in the funding, regulation, or provision of education, but Athenians were nevertheless the most educated people in the ancient world. Independent elementary schools were created in response to public demand, and more advanced lessons followed shortly thereafter, thanks to the travelling professors known as Sophists.

At the elementary level, a common core curriculum[2] evolved naturally from the fact that parents recognized the need for their children to acquire certain basic skills, values, and bodies of knowledge. The range of subjects offered at the secondary level was far more diverse. Apart from a vigorous competition among teachers, however, this diversity produced little friction. It was generally accepted that every student had a right to study what, how, where, with whom, and for how long he or his parents chose.

The most democratic state in history prior to the foundation of the US republic did not require democracy or anything else to be taught in its schools. It did not even require the existence of schools. It did not need to. If anything, its political institutions were made more stable and resilient by its *laissez faire* policies. The freedom and prosperity produced by these policies were so far superior to the living standards of other contemporary cultures that Athenian citizens had a powerful incentive to ensure their city's survival. Political participation was widespread and intense, far more so it seems than in some modern nations. Presented with the obvious fact that their individual security and welfare depended on the security of the entire community, Athenians generally took sensible educational and political steps to ensure the perpetuation of that community.

Even the obvious flaws in Athenian culture were mitigated by its separation of school and state. Though the widespread sexism of the ancient world made it common practice to formally educate only boys, it was not illegal for Athenian girls to attend school. As a result, the philosopher Aspasia was able to open a school and successfully encourage parents to enrol their daughters, after having built a reputation teaching oratorical skills to the city's most famous thinkers.[3] This development was met by consternation on the part of the city's conservatives, but they could do little more than grumble, since traditional discriminatory practices were not enshrined in law. Aspasia's school was a harbinger of things to come. Several generations later, it was commonplace in Hellenistic[4] societies for both girls and boys to attend school.

Athens' chief rival during its golden age was the city-state of Sparta. Spartan schools were also a force for minimizing dissention among the citizenry, but they pursued that aim in a very different way. Every aspect of child-rearing which in Athens was the right and responsibility of parents, was in Sparta the prerogative of the government. State rule, unmitigated by written laws, began before a child was even conceived, and ended only in death. Marriages tended to be arranged by the parents, though the proper age for this decision was laid down by the state (Xenophon 1988, 167). To get the flavour of the relationship between family and state in Sparta, it helps to know the views of the city's most acclaimed leader, Lycurgus, on that most intimate of family matters. According to his biographer, Plutarch:

> First and foremost Lycurgus considered children to belong not privately to their fathers, but jointly to the city, so that he wanted citizens produced not from random partners, but from the best. Moreover he observed a good deal of stupidity and humbug in others' rules on these matters. Such people have their bitches and mares mounted by the finest dogs and stallions whose owners they can prevail upon for a favour or fee. But their wives they lock up and guard, claiming the right to produce their children exclusively. (Plutarch 1988, 26)

This bit of genetic engineering was followed up by a sort of government triage, in which newborn babies were brought before the city elders and inspected for defects. If these elders decided it was better for the state and for the baby itself, the baby was dispatched to a cliff on nearby Mount Taygetus, from which it was thrown (Plutarch 1988, 27).

At the age of seven, all the male children who had passed this test were separated from their families and taken to live in school dormitories

—here again, the education of girls received less attention than that of boys.[5] The way students were treated was well-captured by the terms used to describe them. A class of boys was referred to as a *"boua,"* the same word used for a herd of cattle, and from each herd, a dominant boy was chosen to act as herd-leader. With satisfying consistency, their head teacher was called *"paidonomus,"* or boy-herdsman. This individual was chosen from the aristocracy, and granted the authority to train the boys and to harshly discipline them if any failed to follow his instructions. In his efforts, he was assisted by two "floggers" armed with whips (Xenophon 1988, 168-69; Freeman 1904, 18). Parents had no direct say in the education or upbringing of their children, having to cede their responsibilities and desires to this single, monolithic state system.

Sparta's brutal state school system did produce a very effective military, and its totalitarian ability to homogenize children kept dissention within the populace to a minimum, but it achieved these ends at the expense of virtually every human freedom we take for granted today. It is hard to imagine any citizen of a modern democracy preferring the Spartan approach to community harmony to the Athenian approach.

From the sixth through the eleventh centuries, when Western monarchs could barely sign their own names (Nakosteen 1964, vii), Muslims, Jews, and Christians preserved and advanced classical knowledge in intellectual centres across the Middle-East. At its pinnacle in the tenth and eleventh centuries, Islamic scholarship was a rich mixture of Eastern and Western legacies combined with new work in mathematics, physics, and the life sciences.

Before the birth of the prophet Mohammed around the year 570, many children in Persia (now Iran) were already attending elementary schools reminiscent of those of Athens. They learned basic grammar and arithmetic, usually in the teacher's home, and occasionally also poetry, horsemanship, or swimming. Once Islam took hold in the seventh century, however, a new form of elementary education grew up beside the first, in which the Koran became the central, sometimes the only, subject of instruction (Shalaby 1979, 16-23). These two forms of elementary schooling continued to exist side by side, with many of the secular schools charging tuition, while others, along with virtually all of the religious institutions, were maintained by private charitable grants (Durant 1950, 304, 94).

Though it enjoyed monarchical powers and did not hesitate to use them in many areas of life, the medieval Islamic state initially played little role in education. Artists and scholars were sometimes generously patronized by the caliphs and lesser officials, but there was no system-atic government funding or operation of schools. Just as in Athens and republican Rome, schooling flourished under these circumstances, and a fairly coherent educational system evolved. Education generally reached even the poorest children thanks to the religious and secular grant-maintained schools, and the profound conviction of the time that every child should achieve at least basic literacy and a knowledge of scripture. One modern scholar of medieval Muslim education, presumably un-familiar with the precedent set in ancient Athens, has expressed sur-prise at the success of this decentralized educational market:

> The most astonishing fact about it is that it worked in spite of the lack of [government] organization. Even the rules and regulations were not uniform in most cases. However, the form of the classes and the methods of teaching were to a great extent the same through-out the Muslim world. (Ahmed 1968, 52)

Some of this consistency in techniques was no doubt the result of respect for tradition in what was a very traditional society, but the in-fluence of competition and emulation were also key factors. Muslim scholars, like the Sophists before them, strove to learn from each other's successes, copying the things that worked and abandoning those that didn't. They were driven by the same impetus that exists in any com-petitive market: the desire of consumers to reap the advantages of the latest techniques and discoveries. Those teachers who failed to keep pace with the advances in human knowledge occurring in the Arab world could not have prevented their students from finding other teachers who did.

During its golden age in the eighth through the tenth centuries, the Muslim world enjoyed a level of literacy at least the equal of anything that had gone before. In poetry and philosophy it was hugely prolific, and in the sciences it led the world. A crucial factor in these advances was the existence and widespread tolerance of peaceful disagreement among scholars. While religion was the driving force in Arab society, it was initially viewed as compatible with criticism and secular inquiry. So long as schooling and state were kept separate, skeptics and agnos-tics coexisted with orthodox Muslims, and both in turn were tolerant of the Hebrew and Christian scholars who contributed so much to the early work of translation and teaching. Education historian Abraham Blinderman writes:

Perhaps few other periods in the tragic history of the Jewish people have been as meaningful to them as this period of Judaeo-Arabic communion. The renaissance of Jewish letters and science in Arab lands is a glorious testimonial to the cultural cosmopolitanism of the Arabs at a time when Jews in Europe were being burned as witches, plague-begetters, and ritualistic murderers. (1969, 471-474)

This period of unfettered learning did not last. The power of education as a tool of political and religious indoctrination eventually proved too tempting, and around the middle of the eleventh century Nizam-al-Mulk established state-run schooling. Nizam, the chief minister of sultan Malik Shah, was notable for his interventionist government policies and his religious intolerance. An orthodox follower of the Sunnite branch of Islam, he actively sought to suppress the competing Shi'ah branch and looked askance on Jews and Christians. In keeping with his views, the state schools he founded were designed to inculcate Sunnite orthodoxy and to promote his own partisan political aims (Shalaby 1979, 56-57; Nakosteen 1964, 38; Durant 1950, 308-309). Control over what was taught passed from the hands of the learners to the hands of the rulers.

In seizing the education system as a club with which to bludgeon their opponents, the leaders of the Islamic world extinguished the freedom of thought and speech that had raised their civilization to cultural pre-eminence. What had been a vibrant and diverse intellectual society gradually began to calcify. The practical, research-oriented studies that had occupied so many Muslim physicists and physicians were swept away as revelation displaced inquiry and tradition smothered innovation. Ironically, schools abounded during this period:

As Islam began to decline after the end of the eleventh century, the number of its schools of higher learning increased and flourished. These colleges were, however, almost all denominational schools opened and supported by leaders of various Islamic religious factions. Each denominational college was open, with few exceptions, only to followers of a given sect. Religious and literary studies and Arabic language and grammar dominated the subject matter at the expense of philosophy, science, and social studies. (Nakosteen 1964, 42)

And so it was that schooling, which at first had fed the social and intellectual life of the Muslim empire, eventually poisoned it.

The cases just described are not exceptional. The beneficial social effects of market education and the divisiveness of state-run schools are apparent in both ancient and modern societies, and under both autocratic and liberal systems of government. Even in the putatively free and democratic United States, public schools have been guilty of coercion, discrimination, and oppression. While Bostonian public school promoter Horace Mann was going to great paeans to convince the public that state schools would cure all social ills, other mid-19th-century advocates focused on one "ill" in particular: immigration.

The majority of New England's political and educational leaders was Anglo-Saxon and Protestant, as was most of the population. The society was to a great extent homogeneous and many people preferred it that way. The ever-mounting waves of immigration of the eighteen-thirties through the eighteen-fifties, particularly the influx of Irish Catholics,[6] were thus seen as a grave threat. Advocates of state schooling were quick to point out that a carefully crafted, government-approved education would go a long way towards ridding recent immigrants of their offensively different customs; producing a sort of stone-washed immigrant graduate with no sharp edges or strong fibres. Typical of this new argument was an article in *The Massachusetts Teacher*, published in 1851, concerning itself with the Irish-Catholic immigration "problem." In a twisted foreshadowing of the sonnet that would grace the Statue of Liberty, it stated that:

> The poor, the oppressed, and, worse than all, the *ignorant* of the old world, have found a rapid and almost a free passage to the new ... The constantly increasing influx of foreigners during the last ten years has been, and continues to be, a cause of serious alarm to the most intelligent of our own people ... Will it, like the muddy Missouri, as it pours its waters into the clear Mississippi and contaminates the whole united mass, spread ignorance and vice, crime and disease, through our native population? Or can we, by any process, not only preserve ourselves from the threatened demoralization but improve and purify and make valuable this new element which is thus forced upon us, and which we cannot shut out if we would?
> (Coulson 1999, 79)

Naturally, the process in question was public schooling. According to the remainder of the article, it was crucial that government education be imposed through "stringent legislation" and "an efficient police" on immigrants regardless of their wishes. This sentiment was one of the main driving forces in the establishment of public schooling in the United States. Nor were Canadians immune to this xenophobia. Egerton Ryerson promised that his universal government school system would prevent a "pestilence of social insubordination and disorder" from being spread by "untaught and idle pauper immigration" (Prentice 1988, 56).

In their early years, public schools did not disappoint the xenophobes. The Protestant Bible was not only freely used in US public schools—to the infuriation of Catholics—but several state Supreme courts ruled that all students could be forced to read from it. Students who refused to read the Protestant Bible could be and were beaten by their teachers, and though a number of parents filed court actions as a result, no teacher appears to have been found in violation of the law for these beatings (Kaestle 1983, 170-171).

When established schools throw the weight of government behind a particular moral or religious view, they inevitably give rise to hostility and frequently to bloodshed within their communities. US public schools have been no exception. When Catholic parents finally won the right to use their own Bible in some Pennsylvania public schools during the 19th century, the city of Philadelphia erupted into what became known as the Bible Riots. More than a dozen people were killed and St. Augustine's Church was burned to the ground.

While the results in this case were extreme, the high level of tension created by public schools was common then and it is common today. Battles between conservatives and progressives over textbooks, the curriculum, evolution/creation, the hiring and firing of teachers, etc. have been going on since the turn of the century and there is no sign that they are on the decline. Though only a small percentage have escalated to violence (sniper fire on occupied school buses, dynamiting of school buildings, that sort of thing) (Jenkinson 1982, 17-23, 22, 18-19), the amount of antagonism they have generated is tremendous. Neighbours have been set against one another precisely because the public schools are owned and operated by the state, and because the policies they adopt affect all citizens, not just those who agree with them.

The record of US private schools is dramatically superior in this respect. It is all but impossible to find evidence of book burnings and demonstrations surrounding the pedagogical choices made by private schools because no one is forced to attend any particular private school.

Parents who believe creationism is a science can find schools that teach it as such, while those who favor evolutionary accounts of human origins can do the same. Neither group forces its views on the other and both are able to live peaceably in the same communities. The students of Catholic schools do not protest the absence of the Catholic Bible from public schools or from Muslim academies because their own freedom is not impinged by those institutions. There is no need for theory when the facts are plain: free educational markets have consistently allowed a harmonious coexistence of different moral, religious, and pedagogical views in a way that government schools have not and, by their very nature, cannot.

Some schools do indeed serve particular ethnic, racial, and religious groups under educational markets, but these schools *do not* precipitate conflicts. Just as churches of many different faiths are able to coexist peacefully in free societies, so too are schools. It is grossly inconsistent to claim that homogeneous church communities are acceptable, but homogeneous school communities are not. Nonetheless, this inconsistent position is widely held, and so it is worth exploring in some detail.

What, for instance, about racism? Is there an advantage to public schools over markets in the treatment of racial minorities? The evidence indicates otherwise. Throughout history, governments have used their established schools to repress members of ill-regarded groups, whether religious, ethnic, or racial. For six decades, the highest court in the United States held that it was perfectly acceptable for state schools to ignore the fourteenth amendment and segregate students by race. Most did. It is true that the majority of independent schools at that time were also segregated, but there was at least the possibility for enlightened non-racists to send their children to independent mixed-race schools—a possibility that did not exist within the government system, at least not in the south.

This disparity is very much reminiscent of the way that the extreme sexism of the ancient Greeks played itself out in the free education market of Athens versus the state schools of Sparta. While girls were prevented by law from attending school with boys in Sparta, Athenian sexism was only a matter of tradition, and Aspasia was able to successfully flout it by opening her own school. Within a few generations, it became commonplace for girls as well as boys to attend school in Hellenistic cities organized along Athenian lines.

Forty years after the US Supreme Court finally reversed itself and struck down school segregation laws, the public education offered to Blacks is still inferior in the majority of cases to that received by Whites. Urban public schools serving predominantly African-American students suffer from extreme inefficiency, pedagogical neglect, and even decrepit and collapsing buildings (Coulson 1999, 209-211; see also Kozol 1992). When compared to private schools serving the same population, many public schools hardly deserve to be called institutions of learning. Urban private schools serving low-income minority students spend far less per student than public schools, are better maintained, safer, enjoy superior classroom discipline, and raise student achievement above the level achieved in government schools (Coulson 1999, 266-273, 279-286).[7]

Though racial integration has been a stated goal of US public schools for forty years, those schools are little more integrated today than they were before the first mandatory busing plan was introduced. Independent schools, by contrast, have become vastly more integrated during the past four decades, and, according to recent research, now offer a more genuinely integrated environment than do public schools.

> In the 1968-69 school year, 93 percent of all independent school students were non-Hispanic whites, 3.6 percent African-Americans, and 3.3 percent of other racial or ethnic groups. Thirty years later, the percentage of African-Americans in independent schools has almost tripled to 9.1 percent, approaching the (12.6 percent) proportion of African-Americans in the population at large. The overall percentage of minority students in independent schools has leapt from 6.9 percent to 22 percent during the same period. Even after this rapid rise, the rate of growth in black independent school enrolment continues to outpace that of total independent school enrolment or white independent school enrolment. (Coulson 1999, 276)

But how much do students of different racial and ethnic backgrounds really interact in private or public schools? Professor Jay Greene and his colleague Nicole Mellow cleverly addressed that question by observing the voluntary seating choices of students in school lunchrooms. This, they reasoned, was a far more meaningful measure of integration than overall district or even school-level enrolment figures. What they found is that students in private (particularly religious) schools were much more likely to choose lunch partners of other races than were students in public schools (Greene 1998, Published on the Web at www. SchoolChoices.org/roo/jay1.htm). Just as integration of the sexes was better achieved under the free market of ancient Hellenistic civilizations, so racial integration is now better achieved by independent schools.

Conclusion

Contrary to popular conception, the preponderance of the evidence shows free education markets to have far more benign effects on their societies than state-run school systems. Though this finding may seem counter-intuitive at first, a single realization is all that is necessary to understand it: Coercion, not diversity, has historically been the cause of balkanization in education systems. Time and again, heterogeneous societies have been able to exist in comparative harmony thanks to the freedom of parents to obtain the sort of education they valued for their children without forcing it on their neighbours. State school systems, by contrast, have consistently been used by powerful groups (whether democratic majorities or ruling elites) to discriminate against weaker groups. In the 19th century United States they were used as a club to beat down Catholic immigrants, and in turn-of-the-millennium Ontario they elevate Catholics above all other religious groups. The social tensions are just as real in either case.

It is certainly possible that the preceding distillation of the historical evidence may leave some readers unconvinced—in much the same way that seeing only the tip of a particular iceberg may have left the Titanic's captain unconvinced. But just as there is more berg than can be seen above the waves, there is more historical evidence than can be related in a single paper. It is my hope that this essay will encourage all sides in the school choice debate to consider the historical precedents when drawing conclusions about the relative social benefits of state school systems versus free education markets.

References

Adler v. Ontario. Internet at http://www.droit.umontreal.ca/doc/csc-scc/en/pub/ 1996/vol3/html/1996scr3_0609.html.

Ahmed, Munir-ud-Din. 1968. *Muslim Education and the Scholars' Social Status*. Zurich: Verlag.

Arnold, Janice. 1999. "Major changes urged to Quebec school system." *Canadian Jewish News*. (6 May).

Blackwell, Tom. 1999. "Ontario's Catholic school funding violates rights: UN, Ruled unfair to other faiths: Province vows to continue with current system." *National Post*. (6 November).

Blinderman, Abraham. 1969. "Medieval Correspondence Education: The Response of the Gaonate." *History of Education Quarterly* 9 (no. 4.): 471-74.

Brown, Louise. 2000. "Ottawa presses Ontario to fund religious schools." *Toronto Star*. (18 January). Online at http://www.campuslife.utoronto.ca/groups/jsu/ news/thestar2.htm

Charter of Rights and Freedoms. 1982. Internet at gopher://insight.mcmaster.ca/ 00/org/efc/canada.charter.

Coulson, Andrew, J. 1999. *Market Education: The Unknown History*. New Brunswick, NJ: Transaction Books.

Durant, Will. 1950. *The Age of Faith*. New York: Schuster & Schuster.

Freeman, K. 1904. *The Schools of Hellas*. New York: Teachers College Press.

Greene, Jay P. 1998. "Integration Where It Counts: A Study of Racial Integration in Public and Private School Lunchrooms." Working paper presented at the meeting of the American Political Science Association, Boston. (September). Internet at www.SchoolChoices.org/roo/jay1.htm

Jenkinson, Edward B. 1982. *Censors in the Classroom: The Mind Benders*. New York: Avon Books.

Kaestle, Carl F. 1983. *Pillars of the Republic: Common Schools and American Society 1780-1860*. New York: Hill and Wang.

McDonald, Neil. 1978. "Egerton Ryerson and the School as an Agent of Political Socialization." In *Egerton Ryerson and His Times*. Quoting Egerton Ryerson. Toronto: Macmillan.

Nakosteen, M. 1964. *History of Islamic Origins of Western Education*. Boulder: University of Colorado Press.

Plutarch. 1988. "Lycurgus." In *Plutarch on Sparta*. Richard J. A. Talbert, tr. New York: Penguin Books.

Prentice, Alison. 1978. "The Public Instructor: Ryerson and the Role of Public School Administrator." In McDonald and Chaiton, eds., *Egerton Ryerson and His Times*. Quoting Egerton Ryerson. Toronto: Macmillan.

———. 1988. *The School Promoters: Education and Social Class in Mid-Nineteenth Century Upper Canada*. Quoting Egerton Ryerson. Toronto: McClelland and Stewart.

Shalaby, Ahmad. 1979. *History of Muslim Education*. Karachi: Indus Publications.

Vu, Uyen. 1998. "Group wants religion taken out of schools." *Montreal Gazette*. (12 July).

Walker, John. 1999. "Eighteenth Annual Report." Montreal: English Speaking Catholic Council Board of Directors. Internet at http://www.qfa.qc.ca/escc/98-99AR.htm

Xenophon. 1988. "Spartan Society." In *Plutarch on Sparta*. Richard J. A. Talbert, tr. New York: Penguin Books.

Notes

1 For greater detail on ancient education, see Coulson, *Market Education*, Chapter 2.
2 Reading, writing, athletics, arithmetic, poetry, and music. Art was later added.
3 Socrates, for example, apparently counted himself among her grateful students.
4 The term Hellenistic world, though literally meaning those societies steeped in Greek culture, more accurately refers to cultures based on Athenian practices, as the traditions of Sparta and other divergent Greek city-states were not widely adopted.
5 Spartan girls were encouraged to train and compete in athletics, however.
6 Especially during the Irish potato famine of 1845-50.
7 See also: Anthony S. Bryk, Valerie E. Lee, and Peter B. Holland, *Catholic Schools and the Common Good* (Cambridge, MA: Harvard University Press, 1993). And: Jay P. Greene, Paul E. Peterson, Jiangtao Du, Leesa Boeger, and Curtis L. Frazier, "The Effectiveness of School Choice in Milwaukee: A Secondary Analysis of Data from the Program's Evaluation." Harvard University Occasional Paper 96-3/August 1996. And: Weinschrott, David J., and Sally B. Kilgore. "Educational Choice Charitable Trust: An Experiment in School Choice." Hudson Briefing Paper no. 189, The Hudson Institute, Special Report on School Choice, 1996. And: Fuller, Howard L. "New Research Bolsters Case for School Choice," Wall Street Journal, January 21, 1997. And: Coleman, James, and Thomas Hoffer. Public and Private High-Schools: The Impact of Communities. New York: Basic Books, 1987. And: James Coleman, Thomas Hoffer, and Sally Kilgore. *High School Achievement* (New York: Basic Books, 1982).

Case Studies in Market Education

Analyzing School Choice Reforms That Use America's Traditional Forms of Parental Choice

CAROLINE M. HOXBY

The majority of the states in the United States are currently considering, or have recently passed reforms, that increase the ease with which parents may choose schools for their children.[1] At first view these reforms seem to take elementary and secondary education into wholly unknown territory. Yet this view neglects the fact that choices made by American parents have traditionally been an important force in determining the education their children receive. Parents' ability to choose among fiscally independent public school districts (through residential decisions) and to choose private schools (by paying tuition) are such an established feature of American education that they are almost taken for granted. Yet through these choices American parents exercise more control over their children's schooling than do many of their European counterparts.[2] However, American parents are not all equally able to exercise choice. High-income parents routinely exercise more choice than low-income parents because high-income parents have more school districts and private schools within their choice set. Moreover, there is significant variation in the degree of choice across different areas of the

The author gratefully acknowledges helpful comments from Nathan Glazer, Bryan Hassel, Paul Hill, Lawrence Katz, and Paul Peterson. Ilyana Kuziemko provided very able research assistance for this chapter. All errors are the author's own.

country. Some metropolitan areas, for instance, have many independent school districts and/or a number of private schools.[3] Other metropolitan areas are completely monopolized by one school district or have almost no private schooling.

In this chapter I attempt to answer three related questions. First and foremost, what general facts can we learn by examining the traditional forms of school choice in the United States? In particular we need to understand the relationships between school choice and student achievement, student segregation (along lines of ability, income, and taste for education as well as race and ethnicity),[4] school efficiency, teachers' salaries and teacher unionism, and the degree to which parents are involved in and influence their children's schools. Second, how do the general facts that we garner from traditional school choice carry over to analyses of reforms such as charter schools, vouchers for private schools, and open enrolment programs? Third, what information do we still need if we are to accurately predict the effects of reforms? And what empirical strategies might we use to get such information? For evidence I draw upon previous empirical work included in several studies.[5] Although I briefly sketch the empirical strategy of each study, I do not attempt to present the results or methodology in detail. Rather, my goal in this chapter is to summarize the results and discuss their implications for school choice reforms.

How Analysis of Traditional Choice Informs the Debate over School Reform

Analysis of school choice reforms should begin with the two basic, traditional forms of school choice in the United States, choice among public school districts and choice between public and private schools. These two traditional forms of choice already give some parents a substantial degree of choice, and the effects of their choices are useful for predicting the effects of reforms. Moreover, empirical evidence on how traditional choice affects students is the *only* way we can learn about the general equilibrium and long-term effects of school choice. For instance, there are a few recent or ongoing studies (including one I am conducting) that evaluate charter and voucher schools using randomized "treatment" and "control" groups of students. The studies by Greene, Peterson, and Du and Greene, Howell, and Peterson are excellent examples.[6] Studies like these can inform us about the effects of voucher or charter schools on the students who actually use the schools. Unfortunately, such studies can tell us nothing about the effects that a widespread voucher or charter school policy would have on who attends public schools or how public schools respond to competition. Analysis of the two traditional forms of choice does inform us about these crucial issues. Furthermore, school choice reforms are always layered on top of traditional choice, and households will make different traditional choices as reforms are added.

Traditional Choice Among Public School Districts: Background and Predictions

In this section I describe choice among public school districts. Later I briefly discuss *intra*district choice, a scheme that has only some of the characteristics of choice among districts. A household chooses among public school districts by choosing a residence. The degree to which households can exercise this form of choice depends heavily on the number, size, and residence patterns of the school districts in the area centered around the jobs of the adults in these households. There are some metropolitan areas in the United States that have many small school districts with reasonably comparable characteristics. Boston, for instance, has seventy school districts within a thirty-minute commute of the downtown area and many more within a forty-five-minute commute. Miami, on the other hand, has only one school district (Dade County) that covers the entire metropolitan area. People with jobs in rural areas typically have only one district or a few school districts among which to choose.

Choice among public school districts—as a form of choice—has several important properties. The first is that districts that are good, efficient providers of schooling tend to be rewarded with larger budgets. This fiscal reward process works because conventional American school finance makes each district's budget depend somewhat on local property taxes, which in turn depend on house prices within the district, which in turn depend on how marginal home buyers value the local schools. Rewards for good, efficient provision of schooling can be obtained so long as districts have a significant amount of fiscal autonomy (especially over marginal revenues and expenditures).[7] The fiscal reward process tends to be sustainable over the long term because it depends on decentralized choices. This is in contrast to centralized reward systems—for example, financial or other "merit" awards for successful school districts that are distributed by the state. These tend to be unsustainable because states cannot, after the fact, credibly adhere to processes that reduce (in relative terms) the amount of money going to failing school districts.[8]

The second important property of traditional choice among public school districts is that parents who prefer different amounts of school spending and different types of schools sort themselves into different districts. As a result, each district is more homogeneous than the metropolitan area is in general, and the residents of each district tend to vote for taxes and support schools that approximately fulfil their spending and curricular desires. This means that districts offer differentiated schooling that follows local parents' preferences to a certain degree. In consequence, choice among public school districts creates residential patterns that mirror households' desired levels of school spending. This is in contrast to residential patterns that purely reflect households' incomes or housing desires. Of course desired school spending depends partly on income, but it also depends on how much a household prefers to spend money on schooling relative to other goods or investments. Low-income or minority households are the most likely to be prevented from making reasonably optimal investments in their children's schooling, because their ability to choose residences in more than one district may be severely constrained by their budgets or discrimination.

Another consequence of choice among public school districts is that parents' preferences have some sway over what local schools do. Any given school district's budget is, for instance, allocated more according to parents' preferences (than, say, according to the preferences of school staff members or the state department of education) when parents have more choice among districts. This is simply because, when parents have more choices, school budgets are more elastic with respect to parents' preferences, and therefore policy is more responsive to their preferences.

Evidence of what happens when an area has more choice among public school districts is useful mainly for analyzing charter school reforms and open enrolment reforms. A charter school is a school that receives a charter to educate public school students, receives a "tuition" payment (from public revenues) for each pupil it enrols, and admits students non-selectively or at random. Although charter schools are "public" schools, they are supposed to have a high degree of administrative autonomy and as much fiscal autonomy as a stable tuition payment per pupil can give them.[9] Opening a charter school thus has some, but not all, of the features of creating an additional public school district to compete with the initial district.

An open enrolment program allows students to attend schools in districts outside their districts of residence. Whether an open enrolment program closely resembles an expansion of choice among public school districts depends largely on the financial transfers that accompany transferring students. If an open enrolment program has financial transfers that closely simulate the fiscal pressures of choice among public school districts, the program is a means of intensifying traditional choice among public school districts by reducing mobility costs and allowing many more households to be on the margin between districts. Most actual open enrolment programs, however, do not have financial arrangements that simulate the fiscal pressures of choice among districts. The financial transfer is usually small compared to the receiving district's own average expenditure per pupil. A financial transfer that is only a small fraction of a district's per-pupil expenditure guarantees that the movement of students from one district to another must remain tiny relative to the size of the receiving district—even in the long run. A somewhat perverse financial arrangement that sometimes occurs in an open enrolment plan is that the money that accompanies the transferring student comes wholly or partly from the state rather than from the sending district.

In summary, studying traditional choice among public school districts is helpful for analyzing charter school and open enrolment reforms. All three types of choice give us a general sense of on what bases parents choose among schools, how public schools differentiate themselves given that they are all subject to public scrutiny and public constraints, whether public providers react to competition for students by improving their programs, how the degree of choice among public providers affects parents' willingness to pay for private school alternatives, and how students self-segregate among schools when they can choose but receiving schools cannot discriminate among them.[10] Traditional choice among public school districts is less helpful for understanding charter school and open enrolment reforms to the extent that (1) the financial arrangements of the reforms have quite different properties than traditional choice, and (2) charter schools and open enrolment programs depend on the sufferance or cooperation of local school districts, making them less sustainable than traditional choice.

Figure 1 Percentage of K–12 Students Enrolled in Private Schools, 1960-90

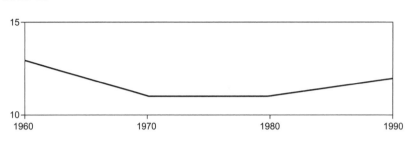

Source: Author's calculation based on data from the US Census of Population 1960, 1970, 1980, 1990.

Choice Between Public and Private Schools: Background and Predictions

The second way in which parents have traditionally been able to exercise choice in the United States is by enrolling their children in private schools. Private school tuition in America is not subsidized by public monies (as it is in some European countries), so parents can afford private schools only if they can pay tuition and also pay taxes to support local public schools.[11] Partly as a result, private schools tend to enrol fewer than 15 percent of American elementary and secondary students. This percentage reached a peak of just under 15 percent in the early 1960s, declined to 10 percent by 1980, and has since rebounded to 12 percent. Figure 1 depicts the percentage of K-12 students enrolled in private schools between 1960 and 1990.

There is tremendous variation in the schooling offered and the tuition charged by private schools in the United States. Approximately 90 percent of private school students attend schools that are affiliated with religious groups, but these include a variety of Christian and non-Christian groups and have tuitions that range from token amounts ("$100 or what parents can pay") to over $10,000. The remaining 10 percent of private school students attend schools with no religious affiliation; these include many of the independent college preparatory schools that charge tuitions of $5,000 or more. More than 65 percent of American private school students attend schools affiliated with the Catholic Church; these vary from modest parochial schools with token tuitions to elite college preparatory schools that compete with the independents for students. The modal private school student in the United

States attends a Catholic school that is parochial or diocesan and charges a tuition of about $1,000 (for elementary school) or $2,200 (for secondary school).

A key feature of American private schools is that they typically subsidize tuition with monies from donations or (less often) income from endowments. The share of schooling costs that is covered by subsidies is larger in schools that serve low-income students, but even relatively expensive private schools charge subsidized tuitions. For instance, Catholic elementary schools, on average, cover 50 percent of their costs with donations from local households, donations channelled through the local diocese, and teachers' and parents' contributed services and goods. (Teachers who are members of religious orders also implicitly subsidize the schools because their salaries are minimal.) Catholic secondary schools are less subsidized: On average, tuition payments to Catholic secondary schools cover about 75 percent of the actual costs of schooling. Even the most expensive religiously affiliated private schools in the United States—those affiliated with the Friends (Quakers)—charge tuitions that average only 80 percent of their costs.[12] Note that schools that serve low-income households and charge highly subsidized tuitions are frequently oversubscribed and must ration school places through waiting lists. Some cities and areas of the United States have significantly larger shares of students in private schools than others. Metropolitan areas, for instance, range from highs of 33 percent of students in private schools to lows of approximately 0 percent of students in private schools. This variation is created by historical accident, the donations available for subsidizing private schools in an area, and the quality of public schools. I return to these sources of variation a bit later.

Choice between private and public schools has several important properties. First, private schools that efficiently offer high-quality education tend to be rewarded by gaining more applicants. At the very least, the larger applicant pool allows a private school to be more selective. More often, a larger applicant pool allows a private school to expand. Symmetrically, public schools that do not offer quality education efficiently are likely to lose students to private schools. The students who are drawn away are, for any given public school, those with the greatest taste for the type of education offered by private schools. A second property of choice between private and public schools is that private schools are likely to have an ambiguous impact on the finances of local public schools. On one hand, an increased supply of private schools tends to draw into the private school sector parents who, had their children remained in public schools, might have supported generous public school spending. This phenomenon tends to decrease voter support for public school spending. On the other hand, an increased supply of private schools draws into the private school sector students who would otherwise have had to be educated at public expense. This phenomenon tends to increase public school spending *per pupil*.

Increased private school availability should change patterns of residential segregation because private school parents who would want to live in districts with expensive public schools if private schools did not exist will be willing to live in less expensive districts. Such changes in residential segregation, however, are limited by the fact that private school parents prefer to live with neighbours who have similar professions, educations, and preferences for other local public goods. For instance, private school parents are unlikely to live with low-income neighbours just to avoid paying taxes to support moderately expensive public schools. Finally, private schools put mild pressure on public schools to pay the same input costs that private schools pay. In particular, private schools are less likely to be unionized and to accept supply contracts for political reasons. If they do not pay union wage premiums and pay competitive prices for supplies, their lower costs indirectly put a little pressure on public schools to be cost efficient. The pressure is small, though, because the fact that private school parents continue to pay taxes to support public schools drives a considerable price wedge between private and public schools with comparable costs.

Evidence of the effects of traditional private school choice is most useful for predicting the effects of vouchers. Some properties of vouchers would be quite similar to those of traditional private school choice: Successful private schools would be rewarded with larger pools of applicants, and the least efficient public schools would most likely lose students. The fiscal impact vouchers would have on public schools is ambiguous, but possibly less positive than the fiscal impact of private school competition on public schools. The difference is that vouchers typically would be funded with monies from the local public schools. Some students who would attend private schools even in the absence of a voucher program would use vouchers: This would have a negative impact on per-pupil spending in the sending districts. However, this effect would be offset by the positive impact on per-pupil spending that would occur whenever a student used a voucher who would have, in the absence of a voucher program, attended the public schools. This positive impact would occur because all voucher amounts proposed thus far have been significantly smaller than per-pupil spending in the sending public school districts. Some of the indirect fiscal impacts of vouchers on per-pupil public school spending would be positive as well. For instance, some parents with a taste for quality education would be likely to remain in districts that they would abandon for suburban districts if vouchers were not available. Keeping parents like these has a positive effect on a district's property prices, and therefore on the tax base that supports public schools.

Interactions between the Two Traditional Forms of School Choice

We expect that the two traditional forms of school choice will substitute for one another to some degree. Parents who are able to choose districts that offer schooling and per-pupil costs closer to their desires will have less incentive to send their children to private schools. Of course, public and private school choice are unlikely to be complete substitutes for one another, because the two sectors function under somewhat different constraints. For instance, parents with strong preferences for religious education cannot satisfy these in the public sector; parents with strong preferences for public schooling cannot satisfy these in private schools.

Similarly, we expect some interaction among the reforms. Availability of charter schools is likely to reduce the use of private school vouchers or open enrolment programs. Logically, the more one reform offers a needed type of choice, the less the alternative reforms will be desired or used. For instance, the less autonomy charter schools have, the more parents will want to use private school vouchers. Also, areas that already have substantial amounts of choice among public school districts or choice of private schools are unlikely to make heavy use of charter school programs or open enrolment programs (unless the latter have perverse fiscal arrangements). Besides, areas with substantial amounts of choice among public school districts are less likely to make heavy use of vouchers. The same cannot be said of areas that already have substantial amounts of choice of private schools. Since vouchers would give an opportunity to transfer to parents already using private schools, vouchers would be highly utilized in areas with high private school shares. The means testing in most proposed voucher programs will attempt to reduce transfers by parents already using private schools.

Table 1 Degree of Choice among Public School Districts
of Illustrative Metropolitan Areas

Metropolitan areas with the most choice among public school districts		Metropolitan areas with the least choice among public school districts	
Metropolitan area	Herfindahl index[a]	Metropolitan area	Herfindahl index[a]
Albany, N.Y.	0.0333	Honolulu, Hawaii[b]	1
Bergen-Passaic, N.J.	0.0346	Miami, Fla.	1
Boston, Mass.	0.0352	Las Vegas, N.V.	1
Middlesex-Somerset-Hunterdon, N.J.	0.0366	Fort Lauderdale, Fla.	1
Pittsburgh, Pa.	0.0368	Daytona Beach, Fla.	1
Riverside-San Bernardino, Calif.[c]	0.0370	Fort Myers, Fla.	1
Monmouth-Ocean, N.J.	0.0377	Albuquerque, N.M.	1
Minneapolis, Minn.	0.0416	Hagerstown, Md.	1
Atlantic City, N.J.	0.0490	Jacksonville, N.C.	1
San Francisco, Calif.[c]	0.0531	Sarasota, Fla.	1
Binghamton, N.Y.	0.0563	Odessa, Tex.	1
York, Pa.	0.0568	Cheyenne, Wyo.	1
Scranton, Pa.	0.0572	Lakeland/Winter Haven, Fla.	1
Johnstown, Pa.	0.0573	Reno, N.V.	1
San Jose, Calif.	0.0576	Boca Raton, Fla.	1
Dayton, Ohio	0.0578	Wilmington, N.C.	1
Allentown, Pa.	0.0598	Ocala, Fla.	1
Anaheim-Santa Ana, Calif.[c]	0.0616	Melbourne/Palm Bay, Fla.	1
Seattle, Wash.	0.0631	Lompoc, Calif.[c]	1
Rochester, N.Y.	0.0638	Panama City, Fla.	1
Phoenix, Ark.	0.0642	Bradenton, Fla.	1

Source: Author's calculation based on U.S. Department of Education, National Center for Education Statistics, *School District Data Book*, 1990.

a   An alternative measure of choice among school districts is the raw number of districts in a metropolitan area. However, this measure favors larger metropolitan areas for any degree of choice. The metropolitan areas with the largest numbers of districts are Greater New York City, 286; Chicago, Ill., 209; Philadelphia, Pa., 166; Detroit, Mich., 117; Boston, Mass., 114; Bergen-Passaic, N.J., 94; Los Angeles, Calif., 82; Monmouth-Ocean, N.J., 78; Pittsburgh, Pa., 74; Minneapolis, Minn., 68; Middlesex-Somerset-Hunterdon, N.J., 68; Tulsa, Okla., 65; Portland, Ore., 62; Oklahoma City, Okla., 59; Dallas, Tex., 59; Phoenix, Ariz., 56; Cincinnati, Ohio, 56; Riverside-San Bernardino, Calif., 55; Cleveland, Ohio, 54; Albany, N.Y., 54; and St. Louis, Mo., 53.

Another measure of choice among school districts is the number of districts per 10,000 school-age persons. This measure favors metropolitan areas that have large land areas for their populations. The metropolitan areas with the largest numbers of districts per 10,000 school-age persons are Bismark, N.D., 11.76; Redding, Calif., 10.02; Burlington, Vt., 9.40; Dover, N.H., 9.08; Glens Falls, N.Y., 8.84; Enid, Okla., 8.16; Atlantic City, N.J., 8.14; Great Falls, Mont., 7.98; Salem, Ore., 7.70; Billings, Mont., 7.63; Pittsfield, Mass., 7.60; Texarkana, Ark., 7.48; Denison-Sherman, Tex., 7.29; Peoria-Pekin, Ill., 7.24; Tulare, Calif., 6.84; Yuba City, Calif., 6.62; and Grand Forks, N.D., 6.56.

b   Hawaii is one school district fiscally, so the school district is larger than the metropolitan area of Honolulu. Obviously there is no school district in the state of Hawaii.

c   California has school districts that have almost no fiscal independence, so it is also virtually one fiscal school district. Therefore, it is somewhat deceptive to describe metropolitan areas such as Riverside-San Bernardino, San Francisco, San Jose, and Anaheim-Santa Ana as having significant choice among school districts.

Evidence on the Effects of Competition among Public School Districts

To determine the effects of competition among public schools, we might compare metropolitan areas that have had long-term differences in parents' ease of choice among districts.[13] Ease of choice depends both on the number of districts in the area and on the evenness with which enrolment is spread over those districts. Choice is easier in a metropolitan area where parents choose among twenty districts of equal size than in an area where three quarters of enrolment falls into one of twenty districts, which in turn is easier than in an area with only one school district. A Herfindahl index based on districts' enrolment shares is a good measure of the ease of choice because it incorporates both these facts—the number of districts and the evenness of districts' enrolment shares.[14] Table 1 shows how much metropolitan areas differ in the degree of choice available among public school districts. The differences are largely a result of historical accident and geography. However, we might worry that districts' enrolments can reflect their success: A highly successful and efficient district might attract a disproportionate share of its metropolitan area's enrolment. It might even attract smaller districts to consolidate with it. These phenomena would tend to make simple comparisons of metropolitan areas with public school enrolments concentrated in a few districts versus metropolitan areas with enrolments spread evenly over many districts biased against finding positive effects of competition among districts.

Formally, the observed degree of choice available among public school districts is possibly related to the school quality experienced by the typical student. To obtain unbiased estimates we need to identify geographic or historical factors that increase a metropolitan area's tendency to have many small independent school districts. We need instrumental variables related to the demand for independent school districts, but unrelated to contemporary public school quality. I use the fact that metropolitan areas with more streams had more natural barriers and boundaries that, because they increased students' travel time to school, caused the initial school district lines to be drawn up so there were smaller districts.[15] This estimation strategy allows me to control for a wide range of background variables that might also influence schools or students. For instance, I control for the effect of household income, parents' educational attainment, family size, family composition (single-parent households), race, region, metropolitan area size, and the local population's income, racial composition, poverty, educational attainment, and urbanness. Because I have good measures of self-segregation

---

Table 2   Effects of Competition among Public School Districts[a]

Variable	Effect
Effect on per-pupil spending	17 percent decrease
Effect on student achievement as measured by test scores	3 percentile point improvement
Effect on student achievement as measured by wages	4 percent increase
Effect on student achievement as measured by educational attainment	0.4 additional years of education
Effect on parents' involvement in students' school careers	30 percent increase in probability that parents visit school annually

Sources: Caroline Hoxby, "Does Competition among Public Schools Benefit Students and Taxpayers?" 1997 revision of Working Paper 1979, Cambridge, Mass.: National Bureau of Economic Research (NBER), 1994; and Caroline Hoxby (1998) "When Parents Can Choose, What Do They Choose? The Effects of School Choice on Curriculum and Atmosphere," in Susan Mayer and Paul E. Peterson, eds., *When Schools Make a Difference,* forthcoming.

a   Consider an increase of one standard deviation in the number of school districts in a metropolitan area or a decrease of one standard deviation in the concentration of enrolment among school districts in a metropolitan area. Note that smaller effects are found for metropolitan areas in which school districts do not have financial autonomy (most revenue is state determined).

by school and school district (for racial, ethnic, and income segregation), I can differentiate the effects of choice on self-segregation from the effects on student achievement and school efficiency.[16]

My best estimates of the effects of competition among public school districts, displayed in Table 2, are gauged in terms of an increase in the Herfindahl index of one standard deviation. This corresponds to a substantial increase in the degree of choice among districts; for instance, it is the difference between having 3 and 13 equal-sized districts or the difference between having 4 and a very large number (100, say) equal-sized districts. An increase of one standard deviation in the degree of choice among districts causes a small (and statistically significant) improvement in student achievement.[17] Students' reading and math scores improve by about 2 percentile points, for instance. However, an increase of one standard deviation in choice among districts causes a large improvement in schools' efficiency. This is because the small improvement in student achievement takes place even though schools lower their per-pupil costs by 17 percent when they face an increase in choice of a standard deviation. What is striking is the opposite sign of these effects: An increase in choice improves student achievement even while accomplishing substantial cost savings. The implications for schools' productivity (the ratio of student achievement to dollars spent) are powerful.

What about the effects of competition among districts on the segregation of students? These turn out to be insignificant for a reason that may not occur to us at first glance. The degree of racial, ethnic, and income segregation that a student experiences is related to the degree of choice among *schools* in a metropolitan area, not to the degree of choice among *districts*. (In fact, the point estimates have the wrong sign for the latter relationship.) In other words, students are just as segregated in schools in metropolitan areas that have few districts as they are in metropolitan areas that have many districts. Households sort themselves into neighbourhoods inside districts; neighbourhoods and schools are small enough relative to districts that district boundaries have little effect on segregation. This result demonstrates how important it is to compare realistic alternatives. The realistic alternative to a metropolitan area with a high degree of choice among districts is not a metropolitan area in which all schools are perfectly desegregated and every student is exposed to similar peers. The realistic alternative is a metropolitan area with a low degree of choice among districts and a substantial degree of segregation among schools.

Choice among public school districts has several other effects worth noting. First, choice among districts and choice between public and private schools are substitutes for one another. An increase of a standard deviation in the degree of choice among districts lowers the share of children who attend private schools by about 1 percentage point (on a base of about 12 percentage points, recall). When parents have more choice within the public sector, they are more likely to be satisfied by their public options and are less likely to choose private options.

A second effect is that when parents have more choice among districts they tend to be more involved in their children's schooling.[18] For instance, an increase of one standard deviation in the degree of choice causes one out of every three parents to visit the school in the course of a year and causes school administrators to say that parents have a more significant influence on school policy.[19] Furthermore, parents appear to induce schools to actually pursue the policies that parents, on average, say in surveys that they want to be pursued: more challenging curricula, stricter academic requirements, and more structured and discipline-oriented environments. For instance, a standard deviation in the degree of choice in a metropolitan area raises the probability by 8 percent that a school's regular mathematics sequence ends in a twelfth-grade course that contains at least some calculus.[20]

Finally, the beneficial effects of choice among districts on schools' productivity depend on districts' having a significant degree of fiscal independence. In states such as California where districts depend almost entirely on state per-student allocations for their budgets, the positive effects of choice on student achievement and cost savings are reduced by more than half. This is probably because successful schools are not rewarded through the property tax or budget process for improving achievement or reducing costs. This result has implications for analyses of reforms, which do not always give participating schools sufficient fiscal independence to allow them to benefit financially from their own success.

Evidence of the Effects of Private School Competition

To determine the effects of private school competition on public schools and public school students, we might compare areas with and without substantial private school enrolment.[21] Table 3 shows the US metropolitan areas with the highest and lowest percentages of students enrolled in private schools. There is substantial variation in private school attendance, even within states. However, low-quality public schools raise the demand for private schools as substitutes for public schools. Therefore, simple comparisons among metropolitan areas would confound the effect of greater private school competitiveness with the increased demand for private schools where public schools are poor in quality. Formally, private school enrolment is likely to be endogenous to (partly caused by) public school quality, and this endogeneity would lead simple estimates to be biased toward finding negative effects of private school competition on public schools.

To obtain unbiased estimates, we need to identify factors that increase the supply of private schools in an area and that are unrelated to public school quality. Formally, we need instrumental variables that shift the supply of private schools and are unrelated to the demand for private schools that is generated by low-quality public schools. I use the fact that a denomination's private schools have more resources with which to provide tuition subsidies in areas that are densely populated

Table 3 Percentages of Students in Private Schools
in Illustrative Metropolitan Areas

Metropolitan areas with the highest percentages of students in private school		Metropolitan areas with the lowest percentages of students in private school	
Metropolitan area	Percentage of students in private schools	Metropolitan area	Percentage of students in private schools
Dubuque, Iowa	33.95	Edinburg-McAllen-Mission-Pharr, Tex.	3.38
New Orleans, La.	28.50		
Honolulu, Hawaii	27.55	Las Cruces, N.M.	4.37
Philadelphia, Pa.	26.74	Brownsville, Tex.	4.56
St. Louis, Mo.	25.67	Lawton, Okla.	4.59
Jersey City, N.J.	24.67	Texarkana, Ark.	4.62
Stamford, Conn.	24.20	Peterville, Calif.	4.88
San Francisco, Calif.	23.81	Orem-Provo, Utah	4.90
New York, N.Y.	23.24	Killeen-Temple, Tex.	5.00
Cleveland, Ohio	22.43	San Angelo, Tex.	5.02
Trenton, N.J.	22.32	Hickory, N.C.	5.05
Wilmington, Del.	22.23	Pine Bluff, Ark.	5.14
Bergen-Passaic, N.J.	21.97	Casper, Wyo.	5.14
Erie, Pa.	21.95	Odessa, Tex.	5.22
Cincinatti, Ohio	21.67	Pueblo, Colo.	5.26
Milwaukee, Wisc.	21.18	Fresno, Calif.	5.27
Baton Rouge, La.	20.96	Fayetteville, N.C.	5.82
Chicago, Ill.	20.58	Sherman-Denison, Tex.	5.88
Green Bay, Wisc.	20.55	Merced, Calif.	5.89
Salem-Gloucester, Mass.	19.89	Yuba City, Calif.	5.91

Sources: Hoxby, "Does Competition among Public Schools Benefit Students and Taxpayers?"; and Hoxby "When Parents Can Choose, What Do They Choose?"

by that denomination. Since religious composition of an area is largely a matter of historical accident, it is not likely to have an independent effect on public school quality. Areas with higher Catholic population shares, for instance, have larger shares of teaching services donated by members of religious orders (worth 30 to 35 percent of costs) and provide larger shares of Catholic school income through offerings (25 to 50 percent of costs). Therefore, denominations' population shares fulfil the conditions for a good instrument: They are positively correlated with the supply of private schools, but are likely to be uncorrelated with the part of the demand for private schools that is generated by public school quality. Catholic population shares provide the best in-strumental variables not only because school subsidies are a relatively high-priority use of Catholic Church funds, but also because Roman Catholicism is spread across the entire United States (it is not all con-centrated in one state or one region) and is associated with many eth-nic groups (unlike some other denominations, which are associated with only one or two ethnic groups).

Note that this estimation strategy allows me to control for a variety of background factors that might be correlated both with the demand for private schools and with public school quality (or public school stu-dents' performance). For instance, I control for the effect of a house-hold's belonging to a denomination. If being Catholic, say, affects a household's demand for public school spending or the achievement of its children, this effect is controlled for (and not confounded with the effect of more or less private school competition). I also control for the effect of certain ethnic group concentrations in an area, for the effect of racial and ethnic homogeneity in an area, for the effect of religious ho-mogeneity in an area, and for the effect of religiosity of an area. Numer-ous other background factors are controlled for: family income, the share of households in poverty, parents' educational attainment, family size, family composition (single-parent households), urbanness, population density, and region of the country.[22]

Table 4   **Effects of Competition for Public Schools from Private Schools**[a]

Variable	Effect
Effect on public schools' per-pupil spending	Approximately 0
Effect on achievement of public school students as measured by test scores	8 percentile point improvement
Effect on achievement of public school students as measured by wages	12 percent increase
Effect on achievement of public school students as measured by educational attainment	12 percent increase in the probability of college graduation

Source: Caroline Hoxby, "Do Private Schools Provide Competition for Public Schools?" Working Paper 4978, NBER, 1994.
a   Consider an increase in exogenous tuition subsidies of $1,000 or an increase in exogenous private school enrolment of 10 percent.

My best estimates of the effect of more competition from private schools, shown in Table 4, suggest that if private schools in an area receive sufficient resources to subsidize each student's tuition by $1,000, the achievement of *public* school students rises. This is true whether the measure of achievement is test scores, ultimate educational attainment, or wages. The effect on mathematics and reading scores is an improvement of 8 percentile points. The effect on educational attainment is an 8 percent increase in the probability of graduating from high school and a 12 percent increase in the probability of getting a baccalaureate degree. The effect on wages (for those who work, later in life at ages 29 to 37) is a 12 percent increase.

Interestingly enough, the estimates indicate that competition from private schools does not have a significant effect on public school spending per pupil. This is probably because the two forces described earlier offset one another. On the one hand, an increased supply of private schools tends to draw into the private school sector parents who, had their children remained in public schools, might have supported generous public school spending. This phenomenon tends to decrease voter support for public school spending. On the other hand, an increased supply of private schools draws students into the private school sector who would otherwise have had to be educated at public expense. This phenomenon tends to increase public school spending *per pupil*.

What about the effects of private school competition on the self-segregation of students among schools? I will not dwell on these estimates because their ability to predict the effects of private school voucher programs is limited. This is because the estimates are based on private schools that have religious affiliations, mainly Catholic schools. In contrast, proposed voucher programs often exclude private schools with religious affiliations and always constrain private schools that accept vouchers to either accept all voucher applicants or accept some random sample of them.

The one thing about the estimates that is noteworthy because it has general applicability is that all the self-segregation effects are very small. This is for two reasons. First, public schools are already quite segregated along lines of race, ethnicity, parents' income, and students' performance. When people attempt to imagine the effect of increasing private school availability, they sometimes conjure up a notional public school that is perfectly desegregated. Possibly the effects of private school competition on such a notional public school would be dramatic. However, even if we could estimate such effects, they would be irrelevant, since actual public schools do not correspond closely to this ideal. The actual self-segregation effects of traditional private school competition are small simply because a large increase in self-segregation cannot be obtained by sorting out an already segregated public school. The second reason that self-segregation effects are small is that an increase in private school competition typically allows self-segregation in public schools to increase slightly while self-segregation in private schools decreases slightly. These effects tend to offset one another.

My best estimates suggest that, if private schools in an area receive enough resources to subsidize tuition by $1,000, segregation along lines of race, ethnicity, income, and students' performance decreases at private schools by small but statistically significant amounts and changes at public schools by amounts that have positive point estimates, but are statistically not different from zero.[23]

Finally, note that both private school competition and competition among public schools tend to hold down input costs. Specifically, both types of competition constrain the salary increases that teachers' unions gain for their members (the union wage premium of 12 percent is reduced by about one-third for a standard deviation increase in competition among districts and by about one-half for a $1,000 subsidy for private schools).[24] This result parallels a standard result from private industry: Increased competition in the market for a product (in this case, the market offering schooling to students) tends to decrease the wage premiums earned by unionized workers and other inputs that are supplied by suppliers with market power.

Intradistrict Choice Programs

Intradistrict choice has been used by a number of large school districts for some time. The least dramatic forms of intradistrict choice are magnet or alternative schools to which students typically apply based on their preference for alternative curricula or schooling environments. In the more dramatic forms of intradistrict choice (Manhattan's District 4 or Cambridge, Massachusetts), every student must actively express a preference for a school. Intradistrict choice shares some features of the two traditional forms of school choice discussed above. In particular, the fact that parents and students make an active choice is likely to make them more committed and involved in schooling. However, intradistrict choice programs rarely give schools a degree of fiscal or curricular autonomy similar to that they enjoy in independent school districts or private schools. It is important to recognize that a district that gives fiscal or curricular autonomy to a school in a given year has not given the school long-term autonomy unless the district can bind itself not to revoke that autonomy. Such binding often proves to be politically impossible. For instance, intradistrict choice programs sometimes exhibit long-term fiscal incentives that are perverse because the district cannot, after the fact, resist taking money from successful schools and giving it to unsuccessful schools. The gathering of evidence on intradistrict choice is in an exploratory phase. My own work demonstrates only that simple estimates (comparing districts that have intradistrict choice to districts that do not) are badly biased.[25] The bias is caused by the fact that districts do not randomly enact intradistrict choice programs. Such programs are usually associated with the hiring of superintendents who are given a free hand to "turn around" districts that have recently experienced sharp decreases in student achievement. It is difficult to create a control group of schools that form a good comparison for this type of school. Even before-and-after studies do not enable us to disentangle the effects of intradistrict choice from the effects of getting a new superintendent who is paid more and given greater latitude than previous administrators.[26]

Lessons for Reform and What We Still Need to Know

The evidence on the effects of traditional school choice teaches us several lessons that are helpful for analyzing reforms. They are as follows. First, public schools can and do react to competition by improving the schooling they offer and by reducing costs. They are not passive organizations that allow their students and budgets to be withdrawn without responding. Realistic increases in the competition they face produce significant improvements in students' test scores, educational attainment, and wages. Second, public schools' responses do not depend just on whether they lose students; their responses also depend on the fiscal rewards and penalties attached to gaining or losing students. When competition has little fiscal implication, a public school is less likely to react. When cost competition is weakened by a large price wedge (such as that between public and private schools), public schools reduce costs less than they do when cost competition is on a more level playing field (like that between two similar public school districts).

Third, the segregation effects of increasing school choice via reforms are likely to be small because schools in the United States (not merely districts) are already quite segregated. To accurately predict the effects of reforms on segregation, one must consider a realistic alternative, not an idealized public school with perfect desegregation. Fourth, parents who have greater choice are more involved in their children's schooling. Parents' influence on school policy, which is greater when choice is greater, will reflect, on average, their stated preferences for tougher curricula and stricter school atmospheres. Note, however, that greater choice is also likely to make schools more diverse through parents' influence because like-minded parents will be better able to group together in sending their children to the same schools. (I have no evidence on this last point.) Finally, different types of school choice substitute for one another to a limited degree.

Given these lessons, what other pieces of information do we need in order to analyze school choice reforms? Three information deficiencies stand out. Since we know that the fiscal impact of choice is an important determinant of its effects on schools, the financial arrangements of charter school programs, open enrolment programs, and voucher programs will be key determinants of such effects. These financial arrangements often receive little thought, and they are chosen more for convenience and political reasons than because they generate good financial incentives. States that want to avoid perverse financial incentives should consider financial arrangements that purposely mimic the fiscal impacts of the two traditional forms of school choice. In order to estimate the effects of more dramatic fiscal incentives, we will need to observe actual choice reforms made under a variety of financial arrangements.

The second information deficiency pertains to the long-term sustainability of reforms. All three of the reforms discussed create schools or programs that have less long-term autonomy than the schools that compete in the two traditional forms of school choice. Public school districts have indefinite lifetimes and will not have difficulty raising tax revenues as long as parents want to send their children to the schools. Private schools have similarly indefinite lifetimes and can raise tuition revenues as long as they attract parents. Although some charter school laws are written to give a high degree of fiscal autonomy to charter schools, all charter schools must get their charters renewed by the state (at least) and depend on other organizations to decide their per-pupil payments. It remains to be seen whether charters and per-pupil payments are politically maintainable when and if charter schools become successful competitors for the revenues and students of public school districts. Most open enrolment programs have even less inherent political sustainability.

These programs, at least as written thus far, require the ongoing cooperation of local public school districts (the receiving districts almost always must voluntarily cooperate, though involuntary cooperation is sometimes exacted from the sending districts). The voucher programs passed thus far depend on the sufferance of the sending districts, but some proposed programs have made the vouchers less dependent on those districts. Careful analyses of district-level and state-level politics will be necessary for predicting the long-term sustainability of all three reforms.

Finally, traditional school choice gives us only limited information about the supply response we can expect from private schools under a voucher program or from charter schools. Supply responses are estimated in the analyses of choice among public schools and choice between public and private schools. (For instance, giving private schools additional resources that are equivalent to a $1,000 tuition subsidy creates a 4.1 percent increase in Catholic school enrolment—on a base of about 10 percent.) However, proposed charter school programs and voucher programs sometimes take us beyond the range where extrapolation from traditional school choice results is reasonable. Making a voucher of $3,500 available to all poor students, for instance, would produce a long-term supply response that would be difficult to predict, since the availability and long-term horizon would exceed those of current voucher programs (like Milwaukee's) and the voucher amount would exceed that of most current private school subsidies.

Notes

1   For useful surveys of the reforms, see A. Tucker and W. Lauber, *School Choice Programs: What's Happening in the States* (Washington, D.C.: Heritage Foundation Press, 1995).

2   Americans are more residentially mobile than Europeans, but the typical European family can also effectively choose a school for early grades by choosing a residence. The most important reasons that Americans have more choice are the fiscal independence and autonomous curricular control that typical American school districts enjoy. Much of the fiscal independence of American school districts has been eroded since 1950. In 1950 the median America school district raised almost 70 percent of its revenue from a local tax base. By 1990 the median raised only 35 percent of its revenue from local sources. Also note that Europeans may find it easier to make informed school choices because all students take certain national examinations and schools' scores are publicized.

American students take a wide variety of standardized tests (if any); there is heavy self-selection of the Scholastic Aptitude Test (SAT) and American College Test (ACT) tests; and letter grading standards differ substantially among schools. For discussion of the effect of external examinations on the incentives that schools face, see John Bishop, "Signalling, Incentives, and School Organization," Working Paper 94-25, Cornell University, 1994.

3   These points are elaborated later with references to Tables 1 and 3.

4   The word *segregation* is often exclusively associated with racial segregation. I describe segregation along a number of lines, such as ability and income. Segregation can also be described as *student sorting*, a term that encompasses a variety of phenomena such as "cream skimming" or "cherry picking."

5   Caroline Hoxby, "Does Competition among Public Schools Benefit Students and Taxpayers?" 1997 revision of Working Paper 1979, Cambridge, Mass.: National Bureau of Economic Research (NBER), 1994; Caroline Hoxby, "Do Private Schools Provide Competition for Public Schools?" Working Paper 4978, NBER, 1994; Caroline Hoxby, "The Effects of Private School Vouchers on Schools and Students," in Helen F. Ladd, ed., *Holding Schools Accountable: Performance-Based Reform in Education* (Brookings, 1996), pp. 177-208; Caroline Hoxby, "How Teachers Unions Affect Education Production" *Quarterly Journal of Economics* CXI, no. 3, (1996), pp. 671-718; Caroline Hoxby, "Are Efficiency and Equity in School Finance Substitutes or Complements?" *Journal of Economic Perspectives* 10, no. 4, (1996), pp. 51-72; Caroline Hoxby "When Parents Can Choose, What Do They Choose?" in Susan Mayer and Paul E. Peterson, eds., *When Schools Make a Difference*, forthcoming. Copies of unpublished papers can be obtained from my Web site (through www.harvard.edu) or by sending me mail or electronic mail.

6   See chapter 13 (Jay P. Greene, Paul E. Peterson and Jiangtao Du, "School Choice in Milwaukee: A Randomized Experiment" pp. 335-356) and chapter 14 (Jay P. Greene, William G. Howell, and Paul E. Peterson "Lessons from the Cleveland School Choice Program" pp. 357-392) in Paul E. Peterson and Bryan C. Hassel Editors. 1998. *Learning from School Choice*. Washington D.C.: Brookings Institution Press.

7   Note that the fiscal reward process works through the residential decisions of marginal home buyers. If marginal home buyers choose to locate in other districts because district X is a poor or inefficient provider of schooling, all house prices in district X fall in consequence. There is no need for all households to relocate for all houses' prices to affect the districts' fiscal rewards.

8   See Charles T. Clotfelter and Helen F. Ladd, "Recognizing and Rewarding Success in Public Schools," in Ladd, ed., *Holding Schools Accountable*, pp. 23-64.

9   In practice, however, states' charter school laws vary greatly in the degree of administrative and fiscal autonomy that they give to charter schools. Arizona, for instance, probably has the most autonomous charter schools. They report directly to a state board (not the local districts that might suffer from their success), they are allowed to expand to meet demand, and they earn increasing credibility with (and decreasing scrutiny from) the state board if they perform well. In other states charter schools may have little administrative autonomy because they are automatically subject to all clauses of the local teachers' union collective bargaining agreement. In some states charter schools have little fiscal

autonomy because their tuition payments depend directly on the per-pupil spending of the local school districts (so that a successful charter school in a failing district is automatically penalized when homeowners dislike the local public schools). The least fiscally autonomous charter schools are those that must annually renegotiate their tuition payments with their local districts.

10 Public schools must admit all students in their attendance areas. Charter schools and open enrolment schools must admit a random sample from the group of eligible students who are interested in attending.

11 There are and have been some public subsidies for private school expenses, including small tuition tax deductions and credits. Minnesota currently has a tax credit for non-tuition private schooling expenses. Some states also require local public districts to provide certain textbooks and bus transportation to private school students.

12 Although tuition understates the true costs of private schooling, private schooling does cost significantly less than public schooling on average. Over the entire period from 1976 to the present, per-pupil costs in private schools have always been between 50 and 60 percent of contemporary per-pupil costs in public schools.

13 For this section, see Hoxby, "Does Competition among Public Schools Benefit Students and Taxpayers?" (1997 rev.).

14 The notes to Table 1 show two alternative measures of choice among public school districts and explain why the alternative measures are less useful than Herfindahl indexes. A Herfindahl index based on enrolment shares is as follows. Suppose a metropolitan area has J school districts, which we index by $j = 1, \ldots,$ J. . Suppose each school district has a share, s_j, of total metropolitan area enrolment. Then the Herfindahl index is

$$\sum_{j=1}^{J} s_j^2$$

When there is no choice in a metropolitan area because there is only one public school district, the index is equal to 1. As more districts are added and as enrolment is spread more evenly over those districts, the index gets closer to 0.

15 This typically took place about the time of Anglo-American settlement, which varies with the area of the country. Many of the original petitions for district boundaries cite streams as a reason for not extending the district lines further. Streams are by far the most common natural boundaries for school districts. Note, however, that many of the streams that are preserved in boundaries are small and have never had industrial importance. Today many of the boundary streams are of negligible importance in travel.

16 The estimation equations can be summarized as follows. The main equation is of the form

$$y_{ik} = \alpha H_k + X_{ik}\beta + X_k\delta + \varepsilon_k + \varepsilon_{ik},$$

where y is an outcome such as a student's test score or a school's per-pupil spending, i indexes students or schools (depending on the outcome), k indexes the metropolitan area, H is the Herfindahl index that measures the degree of choice among public school districts, X_{ik} is a vector of background variables that describe the student or school (for instance, the race and gender of the student or the homogeneity of household incomes of students who attend the school), and X_k is a vector of background variables that describe the metropolitan area (for instance, its racial composition and size). The two-tiered error structure adjusts the standard errors for the fact that the degree of choice varies only at the level of the metropolitan area.

There is also an implied first-stage equation that estimates the effect of streams on the concentration of public school districts in the metropolitan area. This equation is

$$H_k = S_k\gamma + X_{ik}\kappa + X_k\lambda + v_{ik},$$

where H_k, X_{ik}, and X_k are as above (except that X_{ik} is effectively averaged for the area) and S_k is a vector of variables that measure the prevalence of large and small streams in the metropolitan area. I multiply the Herfindahl index by -1 so that it is a measure of choice rather than a measure of concentration (the lack of choice).

17   I use the term *statistically significant* to refer to estimates that are statistically significantly different from zero using an asymptotic 5 percent level.

18   For this paragraph, see Hoxby, "When Parents Can Choose."

19   Specifically, the measure of parental influence over school policy rises by two-thirds of a standard deviation.

20   Interestingly, an increase in the degree of choice encourages grade inflation, which I measure by comparing students' course grades to their performance on national standardized exams in the same subjects. This suggests that although parents want their children to be exposed to harder "real" curricula, parents are loath to set higher nominal standards for their children—perhaps because local grade deflation might be misinterpreted by colleges in the admissions process.

21   For this section, see Hoxby, "Do Private Schools Provide Competition for Public Schools?" and Hoxby, "The Effects of Private School Vouchers."

22   The estimation equations can be summarized as follows. The main equation is of the form

$$y_{ik} = \mu V_k + X_{ik}\nu + X_k\pi + \iota_k + \iota_{ik}$$

where y is an outcome such as a student's wage or a school's per-pupil spending, i indexes students or schools (depending on the outcome), k indexes the area (metropolitan areas and counties, depending on their urbanness), V is the average tuition subsidy offered by private schools in area k, X_{kik} is a vector of background variables that describe the student or school (for instance, the student's own religion or the racial homogeneity of the school), and X_k is a vector of background variables that describe the area (for instance, its income composition or religiosity). The two-tiered error structure adjusts the standard errors for the fact that average tuition subsidies vary only at the level of the area.

There is also an implied first-stage equation that estimates the effect of denominations' population shares on the tuition subsidies private schools offer. This equation is

$$V_k = D_k\rho + \bar{X}_{ik}\theta + X_k\tau + \omega_{ik},$$

where V_k, X_{ik}, and X_k are as above (except that X_{ik} is effectively averaged for the area) and D_k is a vector of population shares of denominations $m = 1, \ldots, M$ in area k.

23   Income segregation is measured using students' eligibility for free lunches.

24   Hoxby, "How Teachers' Unions Affect Education Production."

25   Hoxby, "When Parents Can Choose."

26   In addition, before and after studies suffer from bias produced by a phenomenon sometimes called Ashenfelter's dip. The bias results from the fact that treatment (intra-district choice) is assigned to school districts that have recently experienced a negative departure from their own history. Since districts typically display mean reversion (return to their historic paths) anyway, simple before and after studies exaggerate the effect of intradistrict choice programs.

The Alberta Charter School Experience

LYNN BOSETTI, Ph.D.,
University of Calgary

The Charter School Debate

Charter schools are heralded by some policy makers as the great promise for public education (Nathan, 1996). Advocates claim that charter schools will revitalize the system by injecting market forces into an "over-regulated, over-centralized public education monopoly with strong allegiance to the status quo and no institutional incentive to improve student performance" (Buechler 1995, 3). The Little Hover Commission (1996) concludes that charter schools can leverage change within the public education system by "acting as a wedge for both external and internal forces." Charter school proponents argue that student and parent demand for the choices charter schools provide will increase and public schools will fight for the flexibility charter schools enjoy (6).

The charter-school concept is founded on competitive-market principles. Proponents believe that if parents select schools which reflect their own values and meet the learning needs of their children, they will withdraw their children from poorly performing or unresponsive schools, resulting in pressure for higher performance and responsiveness in the public school system. Charter schools were never intended to supplant public education but to supplement it through choices for responsive and innovative programs. Their mandates, explicitly defined in their charter, help to define the choices available to parents. In the eyes of policymakers, the successful programs and practices developed at charter schools would eventually be adopted by other public schools to benefit all children (Bosetti, Foulkes, O'Reilly and Sande 2000, 160). The ultimate goal of choice is to provide the best fit between the educational process and the needs of the learner (Boyer 1994). With charter schools, parents, rather than teachers, determine the best fit between educational programs and their children's learning needs. Parents claim the right to choose schools that will educate and socialize their children, and to take responsibility for the consequences of their choices.

Those who argue against parental choice question whether parents are rational or capable of decisions based on clear preferences. They also question whether parents will be able to demand action from local school boards and teachers (Fuller, Elmore and Orfield 1996), or that they can be relied upon to pursue their children's best interests. School choice requires parents to make judgments regarding quality teaching and learning, and to acquire the cultural capital to engage effectively with the market. Real choice also means that when parents decide to remove their children from one school, they will then be able to get their children into a school they prefer (Bosetti, 1998a). These are some of the key issues in debates over charter schools and parental choice.

Charter Schools

Charter schools are autonomous public schools organized by like-minded parents and educators to provide choices in the educational philosophy or mission of schools, in the delivery of education, and in the governance and organization of schools. These parents receive autonomy and flexibility in the governance of their schools in exchange for high levels of accountability in meeting their mandate, for parental satisfaction, and for the enhancement of student learning in some measurable way. Charter schools are non-denominational. They cannot charge tuition fees, exist for-profit, or discriminate in student admission.

Charter school legislation varies considerably from place to place, and the particulars are unique to the province or state that establishes it. In Alberta, Canada's only province with such legislation, charter schools must provide the basic, provincially-mandated curriculum, and students are required to write all Provincial Achievement and Diploma Examinations. They operate on a three- to five-year performance contract based on the terms of their charter. Their charter is approved by the Minister of Education or by the local school board. At the end of the contract, an external evaluation team reviews the school and determines if it has complied with the legal and financial requirements, has fulfilled its charter objectives, and can demonstrate parental and community support. Based on this assessment, the evaluation team may or may not recommend that the school have its charter renewed (Alberta Education, 1996). There is no appeal process to overrule this final decision.

Charter schools, like other public schools, must hire certified teachers, but the Alberta Teachers' Association will not permit charter-school teachers to be part of the Teachers' Association. Charter schools manage their own funding and are eligible for the same per-pupil grants as public schools.

A total of 12 charters have been approved in Alberta over a 5-year period, and 10 remain in operation. To date, few of these charter schools could be viewed as offering truly innovative programs; however, they do appear to be applying a variety of educational approaches in novel combinations (e.g., differentiated instruction, project-based learning, individual program plans for each student, and instruction in foreign students' first languages). They also provide appropriate programs for students who appear to be under-served within the larger education system (i.e., gifted students, street youth, and students in need of English as a Second Language instruction).

The Development of Charter Schools in Alberta

In 1994, the government of Alberta passed legislation for the establishment of charter schools. The government introduced charter schools as an "addition to the public education system," and as sites of innovation that would "complement the educational services provided by the local public system" and provide the "opportunity for successful educational practices to be recognized and adopted by other public schools for the benefit of more students" (Alberta Education, 1996). Charter school legislation was introduced shortly after a national debate on the role of education in the enhancement of Canada's ability to compete in a global marketplace (Economic Council of Canada 1992; Steering Group on Prosperity 1992; Corporate Higher Learning Forum 1990). The outcome of these debates was a call by various federal agencies for Ministries of Education across Canada to establish environments that encourage individuals to take greater responsibility for their own learning and that of their children; for schools to define their mission, to articulate their methods for attaining it, and to assume responsibility for results (OECD; Corporate-Higher Learning Forum). These agencies advocated that "clients" should be able to choose the institution that best satisfies their needs and aspirations, and that there be real differences among institutions.

Given this broader context, the Alberta government responded by regarding education as a commodity in the marketplace, and charter schools were celebrated as a vehicle to advance the goals of accountability, efficiency, and performance, and to empower parents and other members of the community to become more directly involved at the school level (Bosetti, 1998b). The government de-politicized the debate over the goals of education by assuming an arms-length approach to the administration and governance of education, while at the same time maintaining a centralist position in terms of funding, mandated curriculum, and accountability Issues over the goals of education played themselves out at the local level through school choice initiatives.

Along with the introduction of charter school legislation, the Alberta government made other changes to the education system. These changes included more funding to private schools, a reduction by 12 percent d to overall education funding, provincial standardized testing programs and grade 12 diploma examinations, the promotion of site-based management as the preferred model of school management, the requirement of school councils, and the consolidation of school boards from 141 to 68 (Bruce and Schwartz 1997). The desired outcome of these changes was the creation of a public education system that is goal-oriented, service-oriented, and responsive to market forces (Bosetti, O'Reilly, and Gereluk 1998, 2).

The Alberta Charter School Experience

This chapter examines the successes and pitfalls of the charter school movement in Alberta. It is based on the findings of an in-depth, two-year study of nine charter schools (Bosetti 1998b; Bosetti, Foulkes, O'Reilly, and Sande 2000). The study used a multi-method case study approach to document each charter school, and a triangulated approach to data collection, including document analysis of charter school legislation, charters, monitoring and evaluation reports, charter school annual reports, handbooks and brochures, as well as observation in classes, at special school events, at parent and board meetings, and at meetings of the provincial association of charter schools. Semi-structured interviews were conducted with teachers, administrators, and relevant stakeholder groups to determine the problems and obstacles experienced in the establishment of charter schools, the perceived support for charter schools, and the impact of these schools on public education. Questionnaires were distributed to charter school administrators, teachers, charter school board members, and parents to profile the following: who chooses to work in or send their children to charter schools; issues and concerns related to the establishment and governance of charter schools; teacher workload and professional experience; and levels of satisfaction with these schools.

The Impact of Charter Schools

The government's reform efforts, including charter schools, have encouraged public debate about the educational goals, practices, and achievement of schools. Teachers have felt increased public pressure to ensure students score well on provincial achievement examinations. Local newspapers often publish the results of these exams by rank, listing schools based on student performance. There has been a backlash against child-centred, progressive education, and a diminishing trust in the expertise of professional educators. Numerous private schools have emerged that focus on a core academic curriculum, a structured learning environment, preparation for university, and work in a global market. In Calgary, the total enrolment of children in private education has increased from 3,900 students in 1993 to 10,050 in 1999 (Association of Independent Schools and Colleges in Alberta (AISCA), Web Site at www.aisca.ab.ca).

Provincially, students enrolled in private schools comprise 3.9 percent of the total school population, an increase of nearly 1 percent since 1993 (AISCA).

Initially, there were numerous applications to local boards, particularly in Edmonton and Calgary, to create charter schools. The Edmonton Public School Board responded by converting these charter applications to alternative schools in the system. There were only three proposals that the board could not accommodate, and these became the three charter schools in Edmonton. The Calgary Public School Board, however, did not approve any charter proposals. Instead, it took the position that neighbourhood schools ought to be able to accommodate the learning needs of all children. Five charter schools are located in Calgary despite the school board's disapproval. Only one charter school, Moberly Hall in Fort McMurray, has had its charter granted by a school board; all the other charter schools operate under the approval of the Minister of Education.

A Vehicle for Systemic Educational Reform[1]

The strength of charter schools as a vehicle for educational reform lies less in fostering innovation in the public education system (although that has happened in Edmonton) than in providing schools of choice for parents and addressing the diverse values and goals of education. This is due largely to the lack of technical support and adequate funding for charter schools, and the reality that local school boards have no incentive to support charter schools, which they perceive as undesirable competition. Current legislation in the School Act permits public schools to accommodate applications for charters as alternative programs. The establishment of a charter school requires near "missionary zeal" on the part of parents and teachers who benefit from little technical or financial support, and face cumbersome provincial regulations and intense public scrutiny. This stands in stark contrast to the ease with which school boards may establish an alternative program. As a result, charter schools have not yet grown to have a large and competitive share of the public education system. They have, however, garnered incredible grassroots support from parents and educators interested in alternative education and addressing the needs of marginalized groups.

Charter schools are still struggling to define their place in the ever-changing regulatory environment that governs public education in Alberta. Legislative and regulatory disadvantages facing charter schools have helped keep the movement small, and while existing schools effectively address the needs of the groups they serve, they are having little impact on the larger educational community. The lack of technical, financial, and moral support from government and school boards has required charter school pioneers to be very committed in their quest to overcome what at times seems like insurmountable obstacles (Bosetti, 1998a). In many cases, these challenges have resulted in a strong sense of community and purpose. They have united people through a common purpose—defined by ideological beliefs, values, or special needs—to organize and to make their envisioned school of their choice viable.

Charter schools have persisted despite the hostile environment created by some stakeholder groups. For example, the Alberta School Boards Association (ASBA) and the Alberta Teachers Association (ATA) have denied teachers, administrators, and school board members of charter schools full membership in their associations. The survival of charter schools, despite this hostility, may be attributed to their grassroots support, which has enabled them to operate on shoe-string budgets, to demonstrate acceptable levels of student achievement, and to maintain high levels of parental satisfaction (Bosetti, Foulkes, O'Reilly, and Sande 2000). The experiences of these charter school pioneers provide insight into the conditions necessary for such schools to become viable alternatives within the public education system.

Charter School Profiles

Charter schools in Alberta illustrate how well schools of choice can address the needs of a diverse community within a public education system. They offer a range of educational programs
- Three of the charter schools offer a back-to-basics educational program that emphasizes teacher-directed learning, highly structured learning environments, strict disciplinary policies, and a demand for high commitment from parents for involvement in their children's learning.
- Three other charter schools offer a more student-centred approach to teaching and learning, emphasizing differentiated instruction to meet the diverse learning styles of students and the needs of self-directed or motivated learners. Two of these three schools cater to students identified as being gifted.
- One charter school caters to the needs of street-involved youth who have dropped out of school and have been "shut out" of the public education system. It offers an educational program designed to provide a safe environment for these youth so they can acquire a basic education that is focused on life skills and job readiness.
- One inner-city charter school caters to students from a variety of minority groups, many of whom are recent immigrants who require assistance with learning English. The majority of these students belong to Arab-speaking Muslim communities.

- One school focuses on science and technology.
- Another school is based on the Suzuki method of instruction and emphasizes an arts-enriched program.

Reasons for Choosing a Charter School

Parents at Almadina, the school that caters to the needs of immigrants and second-language learners, say that they were marginalized in the public education system and that the public school did not supported their cultural values and beliefs. Their children struggled to become part of the mainstream in their neighbourhood school, were reluctant to reveal their cultural identity, and did not have their educational needs addressed. For these parents, the charter school provides a safe place where their children are among friends, where the school calendar accommodates their religious celebrations, and the discipline policies reflect their values and beliefs. A few of the teachers speak Arabic, which makes the parents feel welcome in the school. It is apparent that for the majority of parents whose children attend this school, who are low-income wage earners and struggle with the English language, the critical factors influencing their decision to send their children to this charter school include cultural familiarity; shared values, customs and beliefs; and a feeling of safety and comfort for their children. For these parents, unfamiliar with the Canadian education system, the school springs out of their social network, and contributes to the social cohesion of their community and the formation of social capital.

Boyle Street Co-op Education Centre, the charter school focusing on the educational needs of street-involved youth is situated in the heart of the community in which the students "hang out." It is housed in the co-operative multi-service community centre where community workers, teachers, and government agencies work together to address the needs of residents in the community. The community is culturally diverse but has common bonds of "poverty, cultural disruption, and discrimination" (Bosetti 1998b, 61). Students learn about the charter school through their social network and through referral from various community agencies. As part of the community centre, the charter school provides a strong sense of community and support for students and improved social connections. The basic ground rules are that students must treat one another with dignity and respect. The teachers and community workers are strong advocates for the young people who do not have parents willing or able to advocate on their behalf. The program is designed to encourage students who have dropped out to start study-ing again and to cope with the burdens of street experience and/or in-ner city experience. The charter school admits only students who are unable or unprepared to attend a mainstream school.

ABC Charter School, designed for children who are gifted, is an-other example of a school that addresses the needs of a group that felt marginalized in the regular public education system. Parents argue that at ABC, their children are happier and their needs addressed through superior instructional methods and a challenging peer group. The char-ter school is closely connected with provincial and local associations for parents with bright children, and serves as an extension of the existing support network.

Parents sending their children to Foundations for the Future char-ter school—characterized by its structured, sequential approach to the curriculum, teacher-centred instruction, a strict dress code, and disci-pline policies—are united not only in their resistance to child-centred, progressive education but also in their strong commitment to a particu-lar approach to teaching and to a conception of the skills necessary to participate in society. This school is viewed as a safe haven from the influences of mass culture, corporate interests, and technology, and it brings together parents with a particular vision of quality education and a desire for their children to achieve academic success.

Choice in Context

Amy Stuart Wells argues that charter schools are a reaction against the "common school," the government's attempt to provide a uniform edu-cation for all students, regardless of their culture, social class, or reli-gious background. The "common school" version of public education assimilates and indoctrinates students into a "narrow understanding of morality, patriotism, and valued knowledge" (4). School boards in Al-berta and other provinces vary in their approach to public education: some insist on the common school approach while others tolerate and even encourage a greater diversity of educational alternatives. In school districts that provide a wide range of alternative programs and alterna-tive schools, there is little need for charter or private schools. For exam-ple, the Edmonton Public School Board offers 26 programs in 96 schools and has only two charter schools. The school district of Elk Island School, a suburb of Edmonton, has included in its public school system a once-private Christian School as a school of choice. The Calgary Board of

Education, on the other hand, has few programs of choice and has had five charter schools in the area. The city of Calgary also hosts the largest number of private schools in the province of Alberta.

The Success Of Alberta Charter Schools[2]

High levels of satisfaction among teachers, parents, and students, as well as steady levels of student enrolment, provide evidence of the success of charter schools in Alberta. The charter school movement has been slow to grow, but a number of charter schools have had their charters renewed and are maturing. Operationally, this growth means that these schools can shift their focus from establishing the school and its policies and procedures, to the professional development of teachers, curriculum development, and refining their charter mandate.

The nine charter schools included in our study (Bosetti, Foulkes, O'Reilly, and Sande 2000, 163) varied in their stages of development and their success. We found that charter schools that demonstrated acceptable to high standards of student achievement, had filled a niche within the public education system (as evidenced by stable student enrolment, high levels of parent, teacher, and student satisfaction, and low teacher turnover) and were healthy, stable, well-functioning schools. Though our study never claimed to evaluate the schools, our profiles suggest that three charter schools fit the category of well-functioning and stable, five are moderately successful, and two are at-risk or in decline. The following are characteristics of each category.[3]

Characteristics of...

Well-functioning, Stable Charter Schools

- Experienced school board with members with a range of expertise and experience
- Clear educational vision articulated in its charter with an indication of how goals and objectives are to be achieved
- Strong school leadership
- Value-added improvement demonstrated in student achievement
- Rich social capital and social cohesion
- Ability to draw upon the resources of the school community
- Ability to fill a niche in the public education system
- Supported by a society, foundation, and/or university

Moderately Successful Charter Schools

- Are able to secure an appropriate school facility
- Report a high level of satisfaction from parents and teachers
- Show slow growth
- Have a narrowly-defined niche and a strong sense of purpose
- Have stable leadership
- Are often former private schools, converted to charter schools
- Were supported by strong advocacy from an external group
- Showed moderately increased value-added student achievement

Charter Schools At Risk Or in Decline

- Were established without the support of an existing association, foundation or society
- Operated on a shoe-string budget
- Had weak educational leadership
- Had an ambiguous educational vision, or unfulfilled vision
- Experienced conflict among members of the school board and/or with school administration
- Managed financial resources poorly
- Failed to demonstrate value-added achievement for students

Student Achievement

Performance results on provincial measures of student learning[4] reveal that students at charter schools are generally achieving at least as well as students in other jurisdictions, and/or in accordance with expectations based on their described learner needs. For example, the government reports the Provincial Achievement Test results, which show the proportion of students in each school who attain the acceptable standard for the grade level and the proportion who achieve the standard of excellence. In the two charter schools catering to the learning needs of gifted students, 100 percent of the students achieved the acceptable standard and a significant proportion achieved the standard of excellence (i.e., 71 percent in one school and 50 percent in the other). Four charter schools have student achievement results that are slightly above the average for their related public school board and the provincial average. The charter school catering to the needs of English as a Second

Language (ESL) and immigrant students has results consistently below the provincial average.

In part, these achievement results can be explained by the targeted group of students admitted to charter schools (i.e., gifted, musically talented, at-risk, ESL students) and by socio-economic factors. The majority of students who attend eight of the ten charter schools come from well-educated families of middle- to upper-middle-income.[5] We studied neither the socio-economic characteristics of families at the school for at-risk students, many of whom no longer lived with their families, nor those of students at the school for ESL students. Parents of charter school students are actively seeking alternative education to what is currently being offered by the public education system and are actively involved in their children's education. Charter schools are only in the early stages of developing appropriate "added-value" assessment measures and other measures that address the impact of the charter-specific teaching strategies or the expanded curriculum that students are expected to master. For example, characteristic of all charter schools in Alberta are small class sizes and a consequent low teacher-student ratio, yet none of the charter schools has been investigating the impact of this provision on the enhancement of student learning.

Teacher Satisfaction

The "missionary zeal" demonstrated by charter school pioneers in over-coming daunting obstacles and their perseverance despite limited financial, moral, or technical support from the government or broader educational community is striking. Teachers work long hours with limited resources, and often for less money than they would earn in the regular public education system, yet they remain satisfied with and committed to their charter school. Teachers embrace the challenge of working in a supportive school environment with like-minded individuals in a school where the educational philosophy resonates with their own. In particular, they report that they feel they can make a difference working in such an environment with small groups of children. Many of these teachers are in their first few years of teaching and have developed deep loyalties to their school and community. Some teachers, however, are uncomfortable with the "temporary" status of charter schools, the lack of long-term job stability, and low salaries. Teachers in charter schools remain un-tenured and on term contracts.

Parent Satisfaction

Parents are very enthusiastic about charter schools and in most cases formed the main impetus behind their establishment. Many have contributed substantial volunteer hours to establish these schools. However, their level of involvement diminishes as the schools mature. Eighty-three percent of parents volunteer in their children's charter school, and 82 percent of parents intend to have their children remain in a charter school. Parents express high satisfaction with the quality of teaching, the safe and caring environment, and the academic challenge their children receive. Parents uniformly report that their charter school is better than the previous school their children attended and that their children demonstrate improved academic performance, self-confidence, and satisfaction in their learning.

Choice and Competition

It is apparent that while new or dramatic educational strategies and programs have yet to emerge from these charter schools, parents and teachers deem them a success. What distinguishes charter schools from other public schools in Alberta is that their educational strategies and programs are uniformly applied throughout the school and are not found only in a particular teacher's classroom or subject area. The explicit charter combined with small class sizes, teamwork, collaboration among parents and teachers, and a supportive and caring environment has culminated in a cohesive community and a deep loyalty to the school.

Alberta's charter school movement has not built the critical mass necessary to create widespread choice and competition among schools or to lead to major changes in the public education system. However, despite its modest size, the movement has had an impact on the larger system. Charter schools have increased awareness among parents and the community that students have different needs and that not all parents share the same values or educational goals. Charter schools demonstrate a new way of creating diverse programs and of governing schools, and they have given great satisfaction to the parents and teachers involved in them. In some instances, charter school proponents have challenged local boards to respond to parents' requests for more programs and to provide programs and services that address the needs of particular groups of students. School districts have provided more explicit school choice, particularly in the large urban areas.

Lesson Learned[6]

Charter school Establishment Issues

Charter school legislation allows people without formal training or experience in education to create and govern charter schools.[7] These educational entrepreneurs are not constrained by the institutional mindset or by current educational trends in the local public schools. In some cases, their innovations are ill-conceived, in others their innovations do not fit the current view of education by the educational establishment. For one or another reason, other public schools are often unwilling to adopt their practices, despite their popularity among parents and the community.

In the schools we studied, the most successful had their charter developed by people with educational (pedagogical) expertise and a proven track record in operating schools. A strong and well-researched educational mission drives these schools. Those charter schools established by people with little expertise in education encountered more difficulties. For example, in the cases where the rationale for establishing a charter school was to prevent the closure of another school—either a small public school or a faltering private school—the schools were less successful. In these cases it was not the charter or pedagogical vision that was driving the school, but rather the desire of a small community of parents to keep their community or independent school open. Also less successful was the school created for a particular ethnic or cultural community. While the school's charter was to address the needs of second-language learners, problems over governance and administration, together with high teacher, principal, and superintendent turnover, detracted from the original charter. This charter school has suffered because the educational program, integral to the charter, became secondary, and it became unclear what education vision was, in fact, driving the operation of the school.

Many of these problems can be avoided by ensuring that charter plans are based on well-researched, sound pedagogical theory and practice, that charter proponents have access to the guidance and support of administrators, and that they have strong support from their community of prospective student families. Once the charters have been granted, charter board members require access to training and support in school governance. Charter schools also require strong educational leadership from a principal experienced both in school administration and in the areas of the charter's focus, whether that be pedagogical strategies or learners with special needs.

A second issue for aspiring charter schools is sponsorship. Charters are granted or denied by the district school board and may only otherwise gain sponsorship through an appeal to the Minister of Education. School boards have often proved unwilling to sponsor any charter schools, so many charter proponents have had to appeal to the Minister for charter status. This resistance from local boards has created a tremendous challenge for charter schools. It delays the establishment of such schools, forces charter proponents to shop around for school boards, and creates tension between local boards and charter schools. In recent years, local boards have rejected at least eight new charter proposals. Local boards also report reviewing proposals to be time-consuming and claim the resources they commit to this process could be better spent helping their own schools. Clearly, the necessity for charter schools to be sponsored by a school board presents a conflict of interest for the board.

Parent Volunteerism

Charter schools reflect a new relationship between parents and the school, and redefine the role of the state in the governance of public schools. Charter schools encourage the goals of education to be played out at the local level through parental choice as well as political debate. This increases family responsibility for many parents. The effect is that all the parents who exercise choice devote considerable time to the selection of a school. Yet the day-to-day operation of the school falls upon a small group of committed, able, and available parents. Charter schools in Alberta have not yet realized their potential for appropriate parental involvement.

Financial Assistance

One of the biggest obstacles facing charter schools has been the difficulty of securing appropriate and affordable school facilities. Due to a lack of capital funding, charter schools report that 10 to 15 percent of their operating budgets are devoted to obtaining school facilities, a cost not borne by other public schools. This absence of capital funding has impaired long-term planning for school expansion, and has affected teachers' salaries and charter schools' commitment to small class sizes. Charter schools do not operate on a level financial playing field with other public schools.

The government has made changes to legislation to provide more financial assistance to charter schools for the lease and renovation of facilities leased from public schools. This new funding has created some incentive for local school boards to cooperate with charter schools by leasing them vacant existing school facilities, which they were reluctant to do in the past. Some charter schools have had to move from one facility to another to accommodate school expansion, to address the increase in lease costs, or to avoid not being able to renew their lease.

Documenting and Sharing New Practices

Charter schools distinguish themselves not only by their structure and governance and the strong commitment of parents, teachers, and students, but also by the originality of their programs. Starting a new school and an innovative program takes time, and often requires additional resources, staff training, and time for planning and reflection. Evaluation is important but it, too, is time-consuming. The government demands that charter schools produce certain documents for accountability, which are intended to help them reflect upon their successes and improve their practices. However, after only three to five years of operation, it may be premature to require that these schools find ways to communicate their success and innovative practices with conventional schools.

Few forums exist for charter schools to share their successes with public schools, since school boards are often hostile to them and do not welcome them either at teacher conventions run by the Alberta Teachers' Association or at functions sponsored by the Alberta School Boards' Association. In addition, the large bureaucracy and limited autonomy of conventional public schools makes the implementation of charter school practices less feasible (Reville 2000).

Imperfect Governance

Legislation for charter schools was introduced in 1994 without a vision of these schools' long-term place in public education and without consideration of the regulatory, technical, and financial support necessary to create an environment for them to flourish. Since 1994 there have been three Ministers and four Deputy Ministers of Education. In 1999,

Alberta Education was amalgamated with Advanced Education into a super-ministry called Alberta Learning. Responsibility for charter schools has moved from being a special assignment, with one person overseeing its development, to becoming 40 percent of another person's assignment, and finally to becoming the responsibility of a regional office response team. In 2000, the response team spent nearly 60 percent of its time on charter schools, devoting the equivalent of one full-time position overseeing nine charter schools.

The continual shifting of responsibility for charter schools within the Ministry has resulted in a loss of focus for the movement as a whole and the failure by the Ministry to create an environment for charter schools to thrive and succeed. Local boards have proven to be the squabbling siblings of charter schools more often than supportive foster parents. Charter schools have been left to create their own support network through a provincial organization, the Association of Alberta Public Charter Schools (AAPCS). In addition, an independent organization has established the Canadian Charter Schools Centre to offer research and professional development resources to these schools.

If charter schools are to fulfil their potential to leverage change in public education, and if they are to develop innovative practices, the government should assume full responsibility for them: it should appoint a body responsible for granting and renewing charters, for monitoring and evaluating charter schools, and for providing them with technical assistance and support. If charter schools were allowed to compete on a level playing field with other public schools, market forces would rouse school boards from their lethargy and create an incentive for them to adopt practices that have proven to work best, or risk losing students to a growing supply of charter schools.

Conclusion[8]

The Alberta charter school experience has provided insight into the relationship between schools and parents, and redefined the state's role in providing public education.

Parents and teachers identify with their charter schools in ways that they have not done with a public school board or with most public schools. There is a nostalgia surrounding the charter school movement in Alberta, reflected in parents' search for a small school community where their children are safe, known to all, and academically challenged. In their study of parental involvement in magnet schools, Goldring and

Smrekar found that parents who choose actively view themselves as different from other public school parents because their choice represents a significant break from the complacency and compromise of neighbourhood schools. There is a mythology of "specialness" that surrounds each charter school community which teachers, students, and parents draw upon and use to build a culture of sentiment, tradition, and practices. The sense of community, trust, and social cohesion are some of the positive outcomes of charter schools in Alberta.

Public education in Canada differs from province to province and often from school board to school board because Canadian communities are so diverse and because legislation permits public funding, in most jurisdictions, to Catholic, French, and private schools. In a pluralistic society, the ideal of a common, comprehensive school may not be feasible. People want to "decide for themselves the kinds of sub-community they wish to live in, if indeed they wish to live in a community at all" (Holmes, 1992, cited in Gaskell, 1999). There is a clear need for educators and policy makers to engage with each other and the public in debates about the goals of schooling, visions of the good society, and the role of citizen choice. Charter schools are an important experiment in the delivery of education in North America. To date, charter schools in Alberta appear to be less about competition, innovation, and educational efficiency than they are about choice and community. That is, they are examples of alternative schools where parents have a direct voice in the governance of the school and which are driven by an explicit mandate defining educational goals and practices.

Parents, teachers, and students at charter schools must be strongly committed to maintaining their charter school against the opposition of school boards and teachers' unions and with little support from the government that legislated them. Charter schools encourage a community to discuss not only its educational aspirations for children but also the educational practices most likely to achieve them. Charters are not just about family choice; they are also about democracy in action.

References

Alberta Education. 1996. *Charter School Handbook*. Edmonton, AB: Alberta Government.

Alberta Education. 1994. *School Act*. Edmonton, AB: Alberta Government. Association of Independent Schools and Colleges in Alberta (AISCA). Internet at: www.kingsu.ab.ca/~aisca/ <http://www.kingsu.ab.ca/~aisca/>

Bosetti, L. 2000. "Alberta Charter Schools: Paradox and Promises." *Alberta Journal of Educational Research*, XLVI (2): 179-190.

Bosetti, L. 1998a. "The Dark Promise of Charter Schools." *Policy Options*, 19(6): 63-67.

Bosetti, L. 1998b. *Canada's Charter Schools: Initial Report.* SAEE Research Series #3. Kelowna, BC: Society for the Advancement of Excellence in Education. Bosetti, L., E. Foulkes, R. O'Reilly, and D. Sande 2000. *Canadian Charter Schools at the Crossroads: The Final Report of a Two-year In-depth Study of Charter Schools in Alberta.* SAEE Research Series #5. Kelowna, BC: Society for the Advancement of Excellence in Education.

Bosetti, L., R. O'Reilly, and D. Gereluk. 1998. Public Choice and Public Education: The Impact of Alberta Charter Schools. Paper presented at the Annual Meeting of the American Educational Research Association, San Diego, CA.

Boyer, E. 1994. "Blending the Neighbourhood School Tradition with 'Choice Within Schools.'" In Hakim, S., Seidenstat, P., and Bowman, G. *Privatizing Education and Educational Choice: Concepts, Plans and Experiences.* Westport, CT: Praeger.

Bruce, B., and A. Schwartz 1997. "Education: Meeting the Challenge." In C. Bruce, R. Kneebone, and K. Mckenzie, eds. *A Government Reinvented: A Study of Alberta's Deficit Elimination Program.* Toronto: Oxford University Press.

Buechler, M. 1995. *Charter Schools: Legislation Results After Four Years.* Policy report. Bloomington, IN: Indiana Education Policy Centre, Indiana University.

Corporate Higher Learning Forum. 1990. *To Be our Best: Learning for the Future.* Montreal: Corporate-Higher Learning Forum.

Economic Council of Canada. 1992. *A Lot to Learn: Education and Training in Canada.* Ottawa: Supply and Services Canada.

Fuller, B., R. Elmore, and G. Orfield. 1996. "Policy-making in the Dark: Illuminating the School Choice Debate." In Fuller, Elmore and Orfield, eds. *Who Chooses? Who Loses?* NY: Teachers College Press.

Goldring, E. and C. Smrekar. 1997. Community or Anonymity? Patterns of Parental Involvement and Family-School Interactions in Magnet Schools. Paper presented at Annual Meeting of the American Educational Research Association, Chicago.

Gaskell, J. 1999. "The Politics of School Choice in British Columbia: Citizenship, Equity and Diversity." Paper presented at the Annual Meeting of the American Educational Research Association, Montreal.

Holmes, M. 1992. *Educational Policy for the Pluralistic Democracy: The Common School, Choice and Diversity.* Washington, DC: Falmer Press.

OECD. 1996. *Innovations in Education.* Issue 1. Paris

LAUSD Charter Evaluation Report. 1998. Cross-Site Report: The Findings and Implications of Increased Flexibility and Accountability: An Evaluation of Charter Schools in Los Angeles Unified School District. LA: WestEd.

Little Hover Commission. 1996. *The Charter Movement: Education Reform School by School.* Stanford: State of California.

Nathan, J. 1996. *Charter Schools: Creating Hope and Opportunity.* San Francisco: Jossey-Bass.

O'Reilly, R. and L. Bosetti. 2000. "Charter Schools: The Search for Community." *Peabody Journal of Education*, 75(4): 1936.

Reville, R. 2000. *Charter School Initiative Report*. Education Reform Commission. Mass.: Department of Education.

Smrekar, C. 1996. *The Impact of School Choice and Community: In the Interest of Families and Schools*. Albany, NY: State University of New York Press.

Steering Group on Prosperity. 1992. *Inventing Our Future: An Action Plan for Canada's Prosperity*. Ottawa: Steering Group on Prosperity.

Wells, Amy Stuart. 2000. *In Search of Uncommon Schools: Charter School Reform in Historical Perspective*. Internet at: www.tcrecord <http://www.tcrecord/>.

Notes

1   This section is based on L. Bosetti (2000).

2   This section is based on the article by R. O'Reilly and L. Bosetti

3   Over time, more of the charter schools are moving into the high-functioning category. However, at the time of the study, three schools fell into this category and three fell into the moderately successful category. The at-risk schools were plagued by financial difficulties, poor management, and an unclear educational vision.

4   Provincial standardized achievement tests are administered annually to all students in grades 3, 6, and 9. Diploma examinations are required for all grade 12 students. The achievement results for grades 3, 6, and 9 for each school are ranked and published in local newspapers.

5   For example, 77% of both mothers and fathers have at least some post-secondary education. Forty-five percent of mothers have a university degree or a professional certificate, whereas 16 percent have only a high school diploma and 3 percent have not completed high school. Fifty-two percent of fathers have a university degree or professional certificate, 11 percent have only a high school diploma, and 4 percent have not completed high school. Fifty-six percent of all households earn an income greater than $60,000, including 20.6 percent that have earnings of more than $100,000. Only 6 percent have earnings of less than $30,000. Parents of students from Almadina (ESL students) and Boyle Street (at-risk youth) are not included in this sample and would affect these statistics.

6   This section is based on Bosetti, Foulkes, O'Reilly, and Sande, pp. 170-175.

7   The majority of charter schools were established by parents and parent groups unhappy with their experiences with the public education system. Many felt marginalized or "shut out" of the public education system because their perceived values, voice, or needs were not addressed by that system. Many of these parents came to the realization that what they wanted for their children was not what the majority of parents in their neighbourhood schools wanted for their children, nor what the local school board was prepared to offer for their children.

8   This section is based on L. Bosetti, (2000), pp. 188-89.

A Survey of Results from Voucher Experiments: Where We Are and What We Know

JAY P. GREENE, *Senior Fellow,*
The Manhattan Institute for Policy Research

When I began doing research on school choice in 1995 there was little solid, empirical information on the subject. At that time there was only one choice program, in Milwaukee, and the data from that program was not available to the research community.[1] Researchers wishing to examine the effects of school choice were limited to collecting evidence from public and private schools and extrapolating to what would happen under a choice system. A leading researcher James Coleman followed this approach and consistently found, after controlling for background differences, that private school students performed better academically than public schools students.[2] Coleman and others also found that private schools, while educating a lower proportion of minority students than public schools, distributed their minority students more evenly, producing racial integration better than that found in public schools. From these findings Coleman and others suggested that providing vouchers or tax credits for families to select their choice of private or public schools would increase academic achievement and improve racial integration in schools.

Many education researchers remained unconvinced by Coleman's argument. Unobserved and difficult-to-measure differences between families that select public and private schools might account for the apparent academic edge that private school students displayed. Unfortunately, there was no way to respond to this objection fully as long as the comparison was between families that chose a private school and those that did not. No matter how many controls were introduced for background differences, it was always possible that some other unobserved factors really explained the differences in outcomes. Many education researchers also remained unpersuaded that school choice would help promote integration. The lower percentage of minority students in private school, critics argued, was a more telling sign of the effect of choice on integration than was the distribution of those students within the private sector.

Without new data, research on the effects of school choice remained deadlocked for many years. John Chubb and Terry Moe advanced innovative arguments, but their work provided more support for a theory of the relationship between school governance and organizational efficiency than direct evidence on the consequences of school choice. Critics of school choice—such as Henry Levin, Amy Stuart Welles, and Peter Cookson—wrote articles and books, but their arguments were largely based on theoretical assumptions, analogies to foreign educational systems, or their particular reading of the debate over Coleman's work.[3]

Starting in 1996, a flood of new data became available, greatly expanding what we know about the effects of school choice. First, John Witte released the data he had obtained on the Milwaukee school choice program to other researchers. Second, Cleveland started the second publicly funded school choice program and made information available to researchers. Third, several privately funded school choice programs were developed, specifically designed to allow for a rigorous examination of their effects. As a result of these new programs and studies, we now know quite a lot about the effects of school choice.

The evidence on school choice can be organized according to three questions:
1) What are the academic effects of school choice on the families that choose their school?
2) What are the academic effects of school choice on the public school system? And
3) What are the effects of school choice on the civic values and integration that we wish schools to promote?

The evidence that addresses the first question, the academic effects of choice on the choosers, is now fairly strong. Our knowledge about the remaining questions is still limited but increasing. Of course, much can still be learned on all three questions, and some people will never be satisfied with the quality or quantity of evidence. But great progress has been made in the last several years in developing a solid empirical understanding of the effects of school choice programs.

It is important to note that, despite some well-publicized disagreements over research findings in recent years, there is a remarkable consensus on the general effects of school choice among the researchers who have collected and analyzed the data. These researchers differ mostly in the confidence with which they draw conclusions and make inferences on shaping public policy, but they do not differ in their general assessments of the programs. That is, all the researchers who served as evaluators of the publicly funded choice programs in Milwaukee and Cleveland—as well as the privately funded programs in Washington, D.C., Dayton, New York, and San Antonio—agree that these programs represent generally positive developments and support their continuation if not expansion. If one relied only on the spin from competing interest groups and the research community on the various evaluations instead of the evaluations themselves, one might easily miss the positive consensus that exists. This positive consensus is all the more remarkable given the issue's politically contentious nature and the rewards for scholars who highlight disagreements with other scholars. As this paper will demonstrate, researchers who have collected and analyzed the new data on school choice largely agree that these programs have positive effects and ought to be continued if not expanded.

The Academic Effects of School Choice on Families that Choose Their School

One indication of the academic effects of school choice is the level of satisfaction with school experience reported by "choosers" as compared to "non-choosers." Here the evidence in support of school choice is unambiguous and overwhelmingly positive. One of the evaluators in Milwaukee, John Witte, reported that "satisfaction of Choice parents with private schools was just as dramatic as dissatisfaction was with prior public schools" (1999, 237). In Cleveland, evaluator Kim Metcalf found that "Across the range of school elements, parents of scholarship students tend to be much more satisfied with their child's school than other parents ... [S]cholarship recipient parents are more satisfied with the child's teachers, more satisfied with the academic standards at the child's school, more satisfied with order and discipline, [and] more satisfied with social activities at the school" (1999, 20). Also in Cleveland, Paul Peterson, William Howell, and I found that, after two years of the program, choice parents were significantly more satisfied with almost all aspects of their children's education than were the parents of a random sample of Cleveland public school parents (1998).[4] Nearly 50 percent of choice parents reported being very satisfied with the academic program, safety, discipline, and teaching of moral values in their private school. Only around 30 percent of Cleveland public school parents report being very satisfied with these aspects of their children's schools. Very similar results were obtained from the privately funded school choice programs in Washington, D.C., Dayton, New York, and San Antonio.[5]

If this were almost any other policy or consumer issue, we would consider the strong positive effect of school choice on parental satisfaction as sufficient evidence to conclude that the program is beneficial to its participants. If, for example, people report that they are happier with the maintenance of public parks, we would consider this as sufficient proof that efforts to improve the parks succeeded. We would not normally feel obliged to count the items of trash and repair problems to verify reports of satisfaction.

The standards for assessing programs in education are different. Many in the education and policy communities seriously consider only changes in standardized test scores and disregard parental reports. These people suspect that parents are stupid and that reports of parental satisfaction are of little value, while test scores are the only meaningful indicator of program success. The bottom line is that, despite the overwhelmingly positive effects of school choice on parental satisfaction, the policy debate has not moved very much.

With the focus on test scores, choice programs have demonstrated some positive effects according to almost all of the evaluations of the five publicly and privately funded choice programs that have been studied. In Milwaukee, Paul Peterson, Jiangtao Du, and I took advantage of the Wisconsin law that requires participating private schools to accept students by lottery when classes were oversubscribed. We compared the test scores of applicants accepted to the choice program by lottery to those rejected by lottery. The test score gains in math and reading, after three or four years of participation in the choice program, were

Table 1   The Effect of School Choice on Parental Satisfaction

Milwaukee

Witte, 1999   "Satisfaction of Choice parents with private schools was just as dramatic as dissatisfaction was with prior public schools."

Cleveland

Metcalf, 1999   "Across the range of school elements, parents of scholarship students tend to be much more satisfied with their child's school than other parents ... [S]cholarship recipient parents are more satisfied with the child's teachers, more satisfied with the academic standards at the child's school, more satisfied with order and discipline, [and] more satisfied with social activities at the school ... "

Greene,
Howell,
Peterson,
1998, 1999

Nearly 50 percent of choice parents reported being very satisfied with the academic program, safety, discipline, and teaching of moral values in their private school. Only around 30 percent of Cleveland public school parents report being very satisfied with these aspects of their children's schools.

Washington, D.C.

Wolf, Howell,
Peterson, 2000

"Forty-six percent of the private school parents gave their school an 'A', as compared to just 15 percent of the public-school parents."

Dayton

Howell,
Peterson,
2000

"Private-school parents are more enthusiastic about their schools than either public-school parents generally or those public-school parents who applied for a school voucher. When asked to give their school a grade from A to F, 47 percent of the private school students gave their school an 'A', as compared to 25 percent of the cross-section of public-school parents and 8 percent of the public-school parents who had applied for a voucher but did not receive one."

New York

Peterson,
Myers,
Howell, 1998

"The percentage of parents "very satisfied" with a private school was significantly higher for all of the following: location of the school, school safety, teaching, parental involvement, class size, school facility, student respect for teachers, teacher communication ... , extent to which child can observe religious traditions, parental support for the school, discipline, clarity of school goals, staff teamwork, teaching, academic quality, the sports program and what is taught in school."

significant for students enrolled in the choice program compared to students denied a spot by lottery (Greene, Peterson, and Du 1998, 345).[6] The gains were quite large, 11 normal curve equivalent (NCE) points in math and 6 NCE points in reading over a four-year period. These gains translate roughly into one half of a standard deviation in math and one quarter of a standard deviation in reading.[7] To put this into perspective, the gap in test scores between white and minority students in the US is about 1 standard deviation.

Unfortunately our confidence in these findings is limited by the missing data caused by high student mobility among poor families and incomplete data collection. The findings after three or four years in the program are based on test scores from 40 percent of the choice students and 48 percent of the control group students. There is, however, good reason to believe that the students whose test scores were missing did not differ systematically from those for whom we had data. After three or four years, our treatment and control groups did not differ significantly from each other in terms of background characteristics collected when they applied, suggesting that little bias was introduced by missing data. They did not significantly differ on their math or reading test scores, their family income, their mother's education, their rate of single parenthood, or the amount of time their parents spent with them (Greene, Peterson, and Du 1998, 344).[8]

We also conducted an "intention to treat" analysis to test for the possibility that selective attrition from the program biased results. In this analysis, all subjects who won the lottery for a voucher were counted as if they were in the choice program—even if they never enrolled or left the private schools to return to the Milwaukee public schools. Because we included scores from these additional students, our conclusions could be based on the results of 63 percent of the choice students and 48 percent of the control group students. The results from the intention to treat analysis were basically the same as those from the main analysis, 11 NCE point gain in math and 6 NCE point gain in reading (Greene, Peterson, and Du 1998, 349).[9] These benefits are roughly comparable to closing the gap between white and minority test scores by one-half and one-quarter, respectively.

Princeton economist and former staff member of the Clinton Administration's Council of Economic Advisors, Cecelia Rouse independently analyzed the data from Milwaukee and arrived at similar results, at least in math scores (1998). After trying several analytical strategies Rouse concludes: "students selected for the Milwaukee Parental Choice

Program ... likely scored 1.5-2.3 [NCE] percentile points *per year* in math more than students in the comparison groups" (1998, 593; italics added). Rouse also writes that her findings for math scores are "quite similar to those reported by Greene et al" (1998, 578). She says that her reading results "are roughly similar to those reported by Greene et al, although they interpret their results differently. Specifically, Greene et al rely on one-tailed t-tests because (they argue) theoretically private school students should perform better" (1998, 580). Another difference between these two studies is that Rouse relies on the test scores of students who sometimes took standardized tests for the wrong grade, given their age, because of fairly high rates of holding students back. We adjusted all scores to be age-appropriate according to tables supplied by the makers of the standardized test. Variations in the practice of holding back students holding back of students in the public and private schools could significantly alter the results.

But discussion of all these differences in analytical strategies obscures a basic point: both my team and Rouse's found that the Milwaukee school choice program had a significantly positive effect on student test scores. Neither study found that students were harmed academically, and both found that there were at least some academic benefits. Even if the teams differ on the full extent of the benefits, both agree that the evidence supports the conclusion that school choice in Milwaukee was academically positive for the families offered the choice to attend a private school.

The third researcher to examine the test score results from Milwaukee was John Witte. Rather than examine the random assignment experiment created by the fact that students were accepted by lottery, Witte compared the academic performance of choice students to a sample of Milwaukee public school students, controlling for a limited set of background characteristics. Based on this comparison, Witte writes: "The general conclusion is that there is no substantial difference over the life of the program between the Choice and MPS students, especially the low-income MPS students. On a positive note, estimates for the overall samples, while always below national norms, do not substantially decline as the students enter higher grades. This is not the normal pattern in that usually inner-city student average scores decline relative to national norms in higher grades" (1999, 236-37). In other words, Witte, relying on non-random assignment comparisons, found that choice did not significantly help or hurt students academically, while two other studies relying on the more rigorous random-assignment comparison found significant academic benefits from choice. If these studies are mixed, as some like to say, they are only mixed to the extent that they are positive or neutral on the effects of choice on test scores.

Despite Witte's finding that choice neither helps nor hurts students academically, he has nevertheless endorsed school choice (Williams 2000, 1). Witte writes, "choice can be a useful tool to aid families and educators in inner city and poor communities where education has been a struggle for several generations." He continues, "If programs are devised correctly, they can provide meaningful educational choices to families that now do not have such choices. And it is not trivial that most people in America … already have such choices" (as quoted in Williams 2000, 1). Thus, all three evaluations of the Milwaukee choice program conclude that choice has some significant benefits for its participants. None of the three find that choice harms students. This is about as close as one gets to a positive consensus among researchers examining a controversial policy.

The Cleveland choice program also offers evidence on the academic effects of choice, but unfortunately the evidence from Cleveland is of low quality because there are no random assignment data nor are there sufficient data on the background characteristics of choice and public school families. Despite these data limitations, some analyses of test scores have been performed by Kim Metcalf of Indiana University School of Education and by myself, Paul Peterson, and William Howell. Both groups find some significant academic benefits to the choice program in Cleveland.

After two years Metcalf concludes: "The results indicate that scholarship students in existing private schools had significantly higher test scores than public school students in language (45.0 versus 40.0) and science (40.0 versus 36.0). However, there were no statistically significant differences between these groups on any of the other scores" (1999, 20). Based on a comparison between one grade cohort of choice students and a non-random sample of public school students, Metcalf's analyses had a very limited set of controls for background differences, which could seriously bias results.

In addition to finding significant test score gains, Metcalf, like Witte, favours the expansion of educational opportunities offered by school choice: "The scholarship program effectively serves the population of families and children for which it was intended and developed. The program was designed to serve low-income students while maintaining the racial composition of the Cleveland Public Schools. ... The majority of children who participate in the program are unlikely to have enrolled in a private school without a scholarship" (1999, 23). Overall, Metcalf has a positive assessment of the effects of the Cleveland choice program on its participants.

Our own analyses of test scores in Cleveland had serious data limitations as well. We had test scores from only two private schools, although those schools did contain nearly 15 percent of all choice students and nearly 25 percent of all choice students who had transferred from public schools. It was possible for us only to compare scores from students over time, relative to how they scored when they first entered these two schools. Based on the experience, described by John Witte above, that over time inner-city students tend to have declining scores relative to national norms, it seems likely that any gains in test scores over time would be a strong indicator of academic progress for the choice students. After two years, students at the two schools we examined had gains of 7.5 national percentile points (NPR) in reading and 15.6 NPR in math (Peterson, Howell, and Greene 1998).[10] These gains were achieved despite the fact that the students at these two schools were among the most disadvantaged students in Cleveland. Our study concluded that, despite the shortcomings of the available data, there were significant academic benefits for choice students in Cleveland.

In Cleveland, as in Milwaukee, all studies of the choice program are generally positive about the program's effects. Metcalf finds some significant test score gains and praises the expansion of educational opportunities the program provides. Greene, Peterson, and Howell also find significant test score gains.

The privately funded programs in Washington, D.C., Dayton, and New York allow for a more rigorous examination of the effects of choice on test scores than the publicly funded Milwaukee and Cleveland programs do. In D.C., Dayton, and New York complete demographic and test score information was collected from all applicants at the time they applied and then a lottery was held to award the scholarships. This complete information on students from the start allows for adjustments to be made more accurately for attrition from the sample that inevitably occurs with low-income families. And the lottery allows for a more rigorous random assignment research design, like that found in medical studies, which compares randomly assigned treatment and control groups.

The test score results from all three of these high-quality random assignment studies are again generally positive. After one year of participation in the program, choice students in grades two through five in New York benefited by about 2 National Percentile Ranking (NPR) in math and reading. Older students, in grades four and five, gained four NPR points in reading and six points in math (Peterson, Myers, and Howell 1998). In D.C., African-American students in grades two through five gained 6.8 NPR in reading, but students in grades six though eight lost 8.2 NPR in math (Wolf, Howell, and Peterson 2000). In Dayton,

Table 2   The Effect of School Choice on Families that Exercise Choice

Milwaukee

Greene, Peterson, Du, 1999	6 NCE point benefit in reading and 11 NCE point benefit in math after 4 years of participation
Rouse, 1998	1.5 to 2.3 NCE point gain in math *per year*
Witte, 1999	Neither benefit nor harm to test scores but "choice can be a useful tool to aid families and educators in inner city and poor communities where education has been a struggle for several generations … If programs are devised correctly, they can provide meaningful educational choices to families that now do not have such choices. And it is not trivial that most people in America … already have such choices."

Cleveland

Metcalf, 1999	6 NPR benefit in language and 4 NPR benefit in science after two years for existing schools
Greene, Howell, Peterson, 1998-9	8 NPR benefit in reading and 16 NPR benefit in math after two years

Washington, D.C.

Wolf, Howell, Peterson, 2000	African-American students in grades 2 through 5 gained 7 NPR in reading, but students in grades 6 though 8 lost 8 NPR in math after one year

Dayton

Howell and Peterson, 2000	African-American students gained 7 NPR in math after one year

New York

Peterson, Myers, Howell, 1998	Choice students in grades 2 through 5 benefited by about 2 NPR in math and reading. Older students, in grades 4 and 5, gained 4 points in reading and 6 points in math after one year.

African-American students gained 6.8 NPR in math but their gain in reading fell short of statistical significance, probably due to a modest sized sample (Howell and Peterson 2000). A National Percentile Ranking indicates how students perform relative to all other students. A student who scores at the 50th percentile is performing better than 50 percent of students on the same test. An improvement of 7 NPR for that student would mean that the student was now performing better than 57 percent of students on the same test.

In all three cities statistically significant gains were observed for choice students and in only one city for one age group was there a significant decline in academic achievement. All of these results were obtained after less than one full academic year of participation in the choice programs (students were tested in March of their first year), so it is still early to draw definite conclusions about long-term effects. Nevertheless, the consistency of positive results across all five choice programs, with eight different evaluations by four different groups of researchers, is striking. It is possible that new studies will find different results. It is possible that over time the gains achieved by choice students will disappear or reverse. But what level of certainty should we require before making reasonable policy decisions? The evidence to date on the benefits of choice for the families that are offered choices is at least as strong, and probably much stronger, than the evidence supporting most public policies.

The Effects of School Choice on the Public School System

If choice helps the choosers, does it do so at the expense of others? The suspicion is that choice programs "cream" the best students from the public schools, draining talent and resources from the public system. On the other hand, it is possible that creaming has already largely occurred in the public system. Higher achieving students and more affluent and involved families may have already chosen a public or private school that suits them, leaving "the rest behind." In fact, the US Department of Education estimates that 59 percent of students currently attend "chosen" schools (1997). But many of the remaining 41 percent lack the financial resources to move to a desired public school attendance zone or pay private school tuition. Can vouchers exacerbate the situation in a way that harms non-choosing families?

As we have already seen, evaluations of the Milwaukee and Cleveland programs have concluded that the programs successfully targeted very low-income families, offering them opportunities that they otherwise would not have. The average income of families participating in the Milwaukee program was US $10,860 (Greene, Peterson, and Du 1998, 344). In Cleveland, the mean family income was US $18,750 (Metcalf 1999, 9). In New York, it was US $10,540 (Peterson et al. 1997, 8). In D.C., it was US $17,774 and in Dayton it was US $17,681 (Howell and Peterson 2000, 40). In Milwaukee, 76 percent of choice students were in single, female-headed households. In Cleveland, the figure was 70 percent. In D.C., it was 77 percent and in Dayton it was 76 percent. The standardized tests of choice students before they started private school showed that they averaged below the 31st percentile in Milwaukee, below the 27th percentile in New York, below the 33rd percentile in D.C., and below the 26th percentile in Dayton. In other words, choice students were generally performing in the bottom third academically. If this is cream, then no one needs to go on a diet.

But all of these programs serve very low-income families because their rules require that recipients must earn less than a certain amount. That is, these programs target and successfully reach very disadvantaged children. Would more creaming occur if the income requirements were relaxed? The evaluation of the program in the Edgewood School District in San Antonio helps address this issue. The program in Edgewood requires only that families qualify for a subsidized lunch, which translates into an income level much higher than that required in other programs. And the Edgewood program offered a generous scholarship to everyone in the district who wished to attend private school, creating unlimited potential for creaming.

If choice programs cream the best students, this creaming should have been visible in Edgewood. It was not. When they applied, the math test scores of the students in the choice program were not statistically different from the average Edgewood student. The reading scores of the choice students were higher, but they were both very low, 35 NPR for the choice students versus 28 NPR for the average Edgewood student (Peterson, Myers, and Howell 1999). (An internal Edgewood School District research report, obtained under an open records request, showed no significant test score differences between those students who took the scholarship and those who remained in public school.[11]) Their family income was the same, US $15,990 versus US $15,939. The percentage living with both a mother and father was the same, 44.8 percent versus 42.7 percent. The mothers of choice students were better educated, but the difference was between an average of 12 and 11 years of

Table 3 Evidence of Creaming?

	Characteristics of Choosers		
	Family Income ($)	Single Mother (%)	Prior Test Scores (NPR)
Milwaukee	10,860	76	31
Cleveland	18,750	70	NA
New York	10,540	NA	27
D.C.	17,774	77	33
Dayton	17,681	76	26
San Antonio	15,990	45	35

education. In short, some differences existed between choice and average Edgewood families but these differences tended to be small, and both groups could be described as very disadvantaged.

The most damaging thing that one could say about these choice programs with respect to creaming is that they probably attract the more capable of the disadvantaged poor.[12] But if this is creaming, then Food Stamps, Temporary Assistance to Needy Families, and virtually all other anti-poverty programs engage in creaming. Anti-poverty programs generally fail to serve the most dysfunctional of the poor because those people have difficulty taking full advantage of the programs designed to help them. This is not normally seen as an indictment against anti-poverty efforts, but rather as an unfortunate reality that all programs face. Like these anti-poverty programs, school choice programs can be designed to target disadvantaged populations, even if they do not always reach the most disadvantaged of the disadvantaged.

Even if choice does not cream the best students, doesn't it drain money from the public schools? It all depends on the program's design. In Cleveland, for example, the state safeguarded the public schools against the financial losses they might suffer from losing students to the voucher program. In Milwaukee, the voucher consisted only of the funds that the state contributes to educate each student, which is about half of the total amount spent by the public schools. Losing students while retaining half of the money normally spent to educate them results in an increase in the per capita expenditure for the remaining students. Of course, there are fixed costs in education, so whether public schools benefit or are harmed financially depends on the extent to which school systems can cut costs when they lose students.

In Edgewood, the scholarship resulted in the district losing as much as nine-tenths of its funding for each departing student because the district was heavily dependent on state and federal money allocated on a per capita basis. The scholarship program operators probably hoped that placing the district's funding in jeopardy would provide incentives for the district to improve its schools in order to retain students. In other words, draining money from the public schools, or the possibility of draining money if schools do not respond to the needs of families, might be exactly what we want. Researchers still dispute whether increasing the funding for public schools without changing the organizational incentives is sufficient to cause school improvement.[13]

From the range of existing and proposed programs, we see that choice could have one of three effects on public school finances: It could take no money from public schools, take some money from schools but increase the per capita expenditure for the remaining students, or threaten significant amounts of money for the public schools if they fail to retain students. The financial impact of choice depends on how the policy is designed, so it is impossible to make a blanket statement about whether or not, or the extent to which, choice drains money from the public system.

In any case, the talent and resources available to the public schools are inputs, not outputs. What is important is whether students and their families, in both public and private schools, benefit from a choice system regardless of how resources are distributed. On this issue, there is less direct evidence available. None of the existing choice programs have been around long enough on a large enough scale to result in much effect, good or bad, on public schools. There are some preliminary indications that public schools are attempting reforms to address the competitive challenge from choice programs. For example, in Milwaukee the public schools have promised to provide individual tutoring to any student not reading at grade level by grade 3. In Edgewood, the district has opened its doors to students from neighbouring school districts to try to offset the loss of students to the privately funded scholarship program. But it is still too early to determine whether these reforms will result in real improvements in the quality of education.

However, a recent study by Harvard economist Caroline Minter Hoxby included in this collection examines the effect of choice on the quality of public and private schools using a very innovative research strategy (1998). Hoxby takes advantage of the fact that some families currently exercise choice by moving to different school districts within a metropolitan area or by paying tuition to send their children to private school. Some metropolitan areas have more choices available than others because some have more school districts and more private schools. For example, Boston has several school districts in the metropolitan area (e.g. Boston, Brookline, Cambridge, Waltham, etc.), while Miami has only one school district for the entire county.

Hoxby examines whether having more choices is related to higher academic achievement. As one would expect from most economic theory and experience about competition and choice, she finds that the metropolitan areas with more choices have higher academic performance at lower cost than do metropolitan areas with fewer available choices. A one standard deviation increase in the available public school district choices results in a 3 percentile point improvement in test scores and a 4 percent increase in wages for students upon entering the work force, all for 17 percent less per capita expenditure (Hoxby 1998, 144). This is a tremendously important finding.

Hoxby goes on to show that a one standard deviation increase in choices offered by the private sector results in an 8 percentile point improvement in test scores and a 12 percent increase in wages for students upon entering the work force, without any significant change in per capita expenditure (1998, 148). Hoxby concludes: "If private schools in any area receive sufficient resources to subsidize each student by $1,000, the achievement of *public* school students rises" (1998, 148). Choice appears to help the non-choosers as well as the choosers.

The evidence suggests that school choice does not cream the best students, does not necessarily take money from public schools, and results in better quality education for public school students by providing their schools with incentives to be more attentive to their needs. Of course, evidence on this last point is limited. It is not available from

Table 4 Hoxby's Findings on the Systemic Effects of Choice

	One Standard Deviation Increase in...	
	Public School Choices	Private School Choices
Test Scores	3 Percentile Increase	8 Percentile Increase
Wages Later in Life	4 Percent Increase	12 Percent Increase
Per Pupil Cost	17 Percent Decrease	No Change

existing voucher programs, but only from the variation in choices available to families in cities across the U. S. The only way to obtain better evidence would be to try some voucher programs on a larger scale to examine their effects on the public schools over time.

The Effects of School Choice on Civic Values and Integration

Even if school choice has beneficial academic effects on students, might it not undermine the civic values and integration that we wish schools to promote? These non-academic outcomes may be as important as the test scores that receive so much attention. After all, the development of a system of government-operated schools was motivated as much by concerns over these civic goals as they were over academic success and economic productivity.[14]

Until recently, there was little empirical examination of this issue. The strongly held assumption that private schools were bastions of segregation and intolerance guided many people's views. Some empirical studies observed that choosers tended to be somewhat more likely to be white and of higher socio-economic status than non-choosers. Of course, even the choosers in existing programs have very low incomes (all average under US $18,750) and are overwhelmingly drawn from minority families (all programs have more than two-thirds minority students and some have more than 90 percent). Nevertheless, from observations of differences between the race and income of choosers and non-choosers, some researchers concluded that choice contributes to segregation.[15] But these researchers ignore the fact that many families already choose their public school by choosing where to live. These residential choices greatly contribute to racial and economic segregation in schools, since public schooling is largely determined by highly segregated housing patterns.

The question is not whether choosers differ from non-choosers; the question is whether offering choices leads to more or less segregation than currently exists under our constrained residential choice system. Thus, the appropriate comparison is not between the characteristics of choosers and non-choosers, but between the segregation provided by systems with more or less choice for parents. Comparing segregation in public schools, where many students have not chosen their school, to that found in private schools, where enrolment is completely voluntary, addresses the question more accurately.

Several studies that I have conducted shed light on this issue. One study examined the racial composition of a random sample of public and private school students' classrooms, collected by the National Education Longitudinal Study (NELS) (Greene 1998). It showed that private school students were significantly more likely to be in classrooms whose racial composition resembled the national proportion of minority students and significantly less likely to be in classrooms that almost entirely consisted of white or minority students. More than a third (37 percent) of private school students were in classrooms with a percentage of minority students that was within 10 percent of the proportion of minority students nationally. Only 18 percent of public school students were in similarly integrated classrooms. And more than half (55 percent) of public school students were in classrooms that were almost entirely white or almost entirely minority in their racial composition, while 41 percent of private school students were similarly segregated. When families chose their schools, as they do in the private sector, more children attended racially mixed classrooms than when families were merely assigned to schools, as they are in the public sector. Choice appears conducive to integration, while government assignment to public school appears conducive to segregation.

In another study colleagues and I observed a random sample of public and private school lunchrooms in Austin and San Antonio, Texas, and recorded where students sat by race (Greene and Mellow 1998). We found that private school students were significantly more likely to be in racially mixed groups at lunch than were public school students. After adjusting for the city, seating restrictions, school size, and student grade level, we found that 79 percent of private school students were in racially mixed groups compared to 43 percent of public school students. Sitting in a racially mixed group was defined as having any one of five adjacent students of a different racial or ethnic group. We found that religious, private schools were better integrated than were secular schools, suggesting that the low tuition typically found at religious schools helped contribute to racial integration. If vouchers or tax-credits further reduced the financial barriers to private school attendance, integration in private schools might be even better.

We also found that public schools with more students from outside their attendance zones, that is, with more magnet program or transfer students, had higher rates of integration. It appears that choice systems, where schooling is detached from housing, are better able to transcend racial segregation in housing patterns. Traditional public schools, however, appear to replicate and perhaps reinforce racial segregation in housing.

In his recent work Stanford economist Thomas Nechyba arrives at similar conclusions about segregation by income (1999). Relying on policy simulations, Nechyba finds, "By removing education-related incentives for high-income households to separate themselves from poor neighbourhoods, vouchers introduce a desegregating force into society. [And] by reducing housing prices in high quality public school districts and raising them in low quality districts, vouchers help more low-income families afford to live in areas with better public schools" (Heise and Nechyba 1999). In other words, the public school system of attaching schooling to housing has created distortions in housing segregation and pricing. Housing prices are artificially high in areas with desirable public schools and artificially low in areas with undesirable public schools, contributing to more severe sorting of housing patterns by income (and race). By detaching schooling from housing, school choice makes it easier for wealthier families to stay in economically mixed neighbourhoods by giving them easier access to desirable schools. And by reducing the premium placed on housing in areas with good schools, vouchers make it easier for poorer families to move into those areas. It is no wonder that vouchers are most supported by poor inner-city residents and most opposed by well-to-do suburbanites.

But these findings are based on examinations of existing private schools or policy simulations. What would the effects of an actual choice program be on integration? Some evidence from the Cleveland and Milwaukee school choice programs addresses this question. Following a strategy similar to that used to examine the data from the National Educational Longitudinal Study (NELS) sponsored by the US Department of Education, I looked at whether choice students in Cleveland were more likely to attend schools that were racially representative of the broader community and less likely to attend racially homogeneous schools than were public school students (1999). I found that nearly a fifth (19 percent) of voucher recipients in Cleveland attend private schools that have a racial composition that resembles the average racial composition of the Cleveland area (defined as having a proportion of minority students in the school that is within 10 percent of the average proportion of minorities in metropolitan Cleveland). Only 5 percent of public school students in the Cleveland metropolitan area are in comparably integrated schools. More than three-fifths (61 percent) of public school students in metropolitan Cleveland attend schools that are almost entirely white or almost entirely minority in their racial composition. Half of the students in the Cleveland Scholarship Program are in comparably segregated schools. The amount of integration is not great in either system, but it is markedly better in the choice program.

Howard Fuller and George Mitchell examined racial integration data from Milwaukee, and their findings were similar to those from Cleveland (Fuller and Mitchell 1999, 5). In 1998–99, they observed that 58 percent of Milwaukee public elementary students attended schools with more than 90 percent or fewer than 10 percent minority students. Only 38 percent of elementary school students at a large sample of Milwaukee Catholic schools were in similarly segregated schools. In 1998-99, Catholic schools accounted for more than half of the growth of choice students in the Milwaukee voucher program.

The public systems in Cleveland and Milwaukee, which largely assign students to schools based on where they live, produce highly segregated schools. The school choice programs in those cities allow families to transcend racial segregation in housing to select a racially mixed school. And families are more likely to pick racially mixed schools when their choices are enabled by a voucher than when their choices are enabled by their ability to purchase housing in areas with desired schools. The point is not whether choosers are more likely to be of a certain group than non-choosers. The point is that a voucher system produces more integrated schools than does the existing, more constrained, system of residential choice.

An even deeper fear among choice sceptics is that private schools will promote intolerance and anti-democratic values. Public schools, by virtue of their public control, are assumed to be more likely to instil these desired civic values in students than are privately operated schools. Theorists, such as Amy Gutmann, Stephen Macedo, and Benjamin Barber, make arguments along these lines but they have little to no empirical support for their claims.[16] And while there has been a considerable amount of research developing reliable measures of tolerance in political science (Sullivan, Piereson, and Marcus 1982), until recently no one has examined whether tolerance differs among people educated by different school sectors.

In the past two years, four studies have been conducted to measure the effect of public and private education on political tolerance. Three studies measure tolerance using a version of the tolerance scale developed by John Sullivan and colleagues and one uses a similar approach. Respondents are asked to identify their least liked group from a list.

Table 5   The Effect of School Choice on Integration

Greene, 1998, analysis of data from NELS:

More than a third (37 percent) of private school students were in classrooms with a percentage of minority students that was within 10 percent of the proportion of minority students nationally. Only 18 percent of public school students were in similarly integrated classrooms. And more than half (55 percent) of public school students were in classrooms that were almost entirely white or almost entirely minority in their racial composition, while 41 percent of private school students were similarly segregated.

Greene and Mellow, 1998, Observation of lunchrooms:

After adjusting for the city, seating restrictions, school size, and student grade level, we found that 79 percent of private school students were in racially mixed groups compared to 43 percent of public school students. Sitting in a racially mixed group was defined as having any one of five adjacent students of a different racial or ethnic group.

Nechyba, 1999, policy simulation:

"By removing education-related incentives for high-income households to separate themselves from poor neighborhoods, vouchers introduce a desegregating force into society. [And] by reducing housing prices in high quality public school districts and raising them in low quality districts, vouchers help more low-income families afford to live in areas with better public schools."

Greene, 1999, analysis of Cleveland choice program:

Nearly a fifth (19 percent) of recipients of a voucher in Cleveland attend private schools that have a racial composition that resembles the average racial composition of the Cleveland area (defined as having a proportion of minority students in the school that is within 10 percent of the average proportion of minorities in metropolitan Cleveland). Only 5 percent of public schools students in the Cleveland metropolitan area are in comparably integrated schools. More than three-fifths (61 percent) of public school students in metropolitan Cleveland attend schools that are almost entirely white or almost entirely minority in their racial composition. Half of the students in the Cleveland Scholarship Program are in comparably segregated schools.

Fuller and Mitchell, 1999, analysis of Milwaukee choice program:

"To ... compare racial and ethnic isolation in choice schools and MPS schools, we identified [racially isolated] MPS and Catholic elementary schools ... Nearly twice as many MPS elementary students were in racially isolated schools."

They are then asked whether they would agree to allow members of that group to engage in certain activities, such as holding a rally or running for elected office. The more that respondents agree to allowing members of their least liked group to engage in these activities, the more tolerant they are said to be.

In one study colleagues and I analyzed responses from the Latino National Political Survey (LNPS), a national sample of adult Latinos (Greene, Giammo, and Mellow 1999). Subjects were asked whether they went to a public, private, or foreign school for each grade, and they were asked the tolerance questions developed by Sullivan. Controlling for a variety of background characteristics, we found that adult Latinos educated mostly in private school were more likely to be tolerant than those educated mostly in public or foreign schools. The effect was moderate, but significant. Latinos who received their education entirely in private school were willing to tolerate the political activities of their least-liked group 50 percent of the time compared to 39 percent for Latinos who never attended private school, all other factors held constant.

Rather than being the bastions of intolerance they are sometimes imagined to be, private schools appear to be more successful than public schools at instilling tolerance in their students. And remarkably this private school advantage on tolerance appears to last into the students' adult lives.

The data from the LNPS reveal other civic benefits of private education. Adults educated in private schools are more likely to vote and more likely to join civic organizations (Greene, Giammo, and Mellow 1999). Receiving all of one's education in private school increased the rate at which the respondents voted by 14 percent and increased the rate at which they joined voluntary organizations by 8 percent. Government-operated schools, which were created to a large degree for this very purpose, appear to be less capable of promoting desired civic values than chosen and privately-operated schools.

Pat Wolf and colleagues conducted a study of college students at four universities in Texas that also collected measures of tolerance and earlier public and private school attendance (Wolf et al. 2000). That study arrives at the same conclusion as the LNPS study: going to private school is associated with *higher*, not lower, levels of tolerance, even after controlling for a host of background characteristics. The benefit of having received all of one's primary and secondary education in private schools is roughly 0.3 of a standard deviation on the tolerance scale, an effect that is fairly large.

David Campbell examined a large national data set of secondary school students that contained a limited set of tolerance items focusing on whether students would tolerate anti-religious activities (2000). These tolerance measures are an especially hard test of whether tolerance is taught well at religious private schools, given their focus on tolerating anti-religious activities. Despite this likely bias, Campbell finds that Catholic school and secular private school students are more likely to be tolerant than public school students. Secular, Catholic, and other religious private schools students outperformed their public school counterparts on other civic measures, such as their experience with volunteering and their willingness to engage in public speaking or write letters on public issues.

Ken Godwin and colleagues also collected data from students who were currently enrolled in public and private schools in New York and Texas and measured their political knowledge, support for democratic norms, and tolerance (Godwin et al. 2001). Measures of political knowledge and support for democratic norms, like measures of tolerance, are well-developed scales based on a series of questions in a survey. The results show that private education has a statistically significant and positive effect on political knowledge and support for democratic norms. The results for tolerance were positive but fell short of statistical significance. The Godwin study, like the LNPS and Texas college student studies, show positive effects of private education on civic values and fail to find negative effects, as many observers would have expected.

It is not entirely clear why private schools promote greater tolerance, political participation, and social involvement among their students. It may be that private schools teach these civic values better than public schools because they are more racially integrated. Some of the expected by-products of integration are greater mutual understanding, tolerance, and social involvement. Indeed, data from NELS show that private school students are more likely to report greater levels of cross-racial friendship and fewer instances of racial fighting than are public school students (Greene 1998). Perhaps private schools are empowered to address the controversial issues raised in the teaching of tolerance and civic values because they are not democratically controlled and do not fear political repercussions. Perhaps private schools simply teach values more effectively than public schools, just as they may teach math and reading better.

Whatever the cause of the higher rates of tolerance, voting, and social involvement of private school students, the fact that these

Table 6   The Effect of Choice on Civic Values

Greene, Giammo, and Mellow, 1999
Analysis of the Latino National Political Survey
   Latinos who received their education entirely in private school were willing to tolerate the political activities of their least-liked group 50 percent of the time compared to 39 percent for Latinos who never attended private school, with all other factors held constant.

Wolf, Greene, Kleitz, Thalhammer, 2000
Analysis of a survey administered to college students in Texas
   The benefit of having received all of one's primary and secondary education in private schools is roughly 0.3 of a standard deviation on the tolerance scale, an effect that is fairly large.

Campbell, 2000
Analysis of a national data set of high school students
   Catholic school students are more likely to tolerate anti-religious activities than are public school students. Private school students are more likely to volunteer and develop civic skills, such as the ability and willingness to write letters and engage in public speaking on public issues.

Godwin, et al, 2000
Analysis of survey administered to 8th graders in New York and Texas
   The results show a statistically significant and positive effect of private education on political knowledge and support for democratic norms. The results for tolerance were positive but fell short of statistical significance.

---

advantages exist is a striking rejoinder to those who oppose choice on civic grounds. The evidence suggests that we need not fear that giving more students access to private schools will undermine the integration or civic values that we expect schools to provide. If anything, the evidence suggests that expanding private education will help promote these civic goals.

Conclusion

Reviewing the recent evidence on the effects of school choice leaves us with a few basic conclusions:
   • There is consensus among all eight studies, conducted on five existing choice programs by four different groups of researchers that

choice is beneficial. To be sure, differences exist among these studies, but all have found important benefits of choice for the families
that participate in choice programs.

- Choice does not appear to "cream" the best students. In all studies
of existing choice programs, the evidence shows that participants
have very low family incomes, predominantly come from single-
mother households, and have a prior record of low academic
performance.

- The existing choice programs are not large enough nor have they
operated long enough to reveal much about their effects, positive
or negative, on the public school system. However, Hoxby's work
finds that metropolitan areas with more choices available have significantly better outcomes at lower cost. From this examination of
the long-standing residential choice system, we can expect that
choice is likely to improve public schools.

- Private schools are more likely to be integrated (having a racial composition that resembles the composition of the broader community) and less likely to be segregated (having a racial composition
that is almost all white or almost all minority) than are public
schools.

- Private schools are more likely to promote tolerance, voting, and
social involvement than are public schools.

The finding of positive effects of choice on its participants is remarkably consistent across all studies of existing choice programs and
is evidence in which we should have reasonably high confidence. The
absence of creaming is another finding that is consistent across all studies
of existing choice programs and is evidence in which we should have
confidence. The conclusion about the positive effects of choice on public schools is based on an innovative study, but it is only one study. The
best current evidence supports the view that choice should help improve public schools, but we cannot know this with greater confidence
unless we are willing to try more choice programs on a larger scale.

The findings that choice contributes to higher levels of racial integration and civic values are consistent across several studies with appropriate analytical designs. These conclusions are so at odds with
conventional wisdom on the matter, however, that they probably need
additional studies to confirm the results with higher confidence. Yet,
they are the most solid conclusions we can draw given the available
evidence.

But perhaps the most striking finding from the review of school choice research is the absence of evidence about how school choice harms students or society. Given that vouchers cost about half as much as conventional public education, the absence of harm is proof enough that school choice is an attractive option.[17] Perhaps we will detect significant damage caused by school choice or perhaps the benefits we have detected will diminish when programs are attempted on a larger scale. Without attempting large scale programs, we will have a hard time knowing.

References

Campbell, David. 2000. "Making Democratic Education Work: Schools, Social Capital and Civic Education." Paper presented at the Conference on Charter Schools, Vouchers, and Public Education, Harvard University (March 9-10).

Godwin, Kenneth, Carrie Ausbrooks, and Valerie Martinez. 2001. "Teaching Tolerance in Private and Public Schools." Phi Delta Kappan (March).

Howard Fuller and George Mitchell, "The Impact of School Choice on Racial and Ethnic Enrollment in Milwaukee Private Schools," Marquette University, Current Education Issues, Number 99-5, December 1999. See also Howard Fuller and George Mitchell, The Impact of School Choice on Integration in Milwaukee Private Schools," Marquette University, Current Education Issues, Number 2000-2, June 2000.

Greene, Jay P. 1998. "Civic Values in Public and Private Schools." In *Learning From School Choice*. Washington, D.C.: Brookings Press.

Greene, Jay P., and Nicole Mellow. 1998. "Integration Where It Counts: A Study of Racial Integration in Public and Private School Lunchrooms." Public Policy Clinic Working Paper. Internet at http://www.la.utexas.edu/research/ppc/lunch.html.

Greene, Jay P., Paul E. Peterson, and Jiangtao Du. 1998. "School Choice in Milwaukee: A Randomized Experiment." In Peterson and Hassel, eds., *Learning From School Choice*. Washington, D.C.: Brookings Press.

Greene, Jay P. 1999. "The Racial, Economic, and Religious Context of Parental Choice in Cleveland." Paper presented a the Association for Public Policy Analysis and Management. Washington, D.C., (November). Internet at http://hdc-www.harvard.edu/pepg/index.htm.

Greene, Jay P., Joseph Giammo, and Nicole Mellow. 1999. "The Effect of Private Education on Political Participation, Social Capital and Tolerance: An Examination of the Latino National Political Survey." *The Georgetown Public Policy Review* 5 (no.1): 53-74.

Heise, Michael, and Thomas Nechyba. 1999. "School Finance Reform: A Case for Vouchers." Center for Civic Innovation, The Manhattan Institute for Public Policy Research, Civic Report, No. 9 (October).

Howell, William G., and Paul E. Peterson. 2000. "School Choice in Dayton, OH: An Evaluation After One Year." Working Paper, Table 17, Harvard Program on Education Policy and Governance. Internet at http://hdc-www.harvard.edu/pepg/index.htm.

Hoxby, Caroline M. 1998. "Analyzing School Choice Reforms that Use America's Traditional Forms of Parental Choice." In Peterson and Hassel, eds., *Learning from School Choice*. Washington, D.C.: Brookings Press.

Metcalf, Kim K. 1999. "Evaluation of the Cleveland Scholarship and Tutoring Program, 1996-1999." Unpublished manuscript, Indiana University.

Nechyba, Thomas. 1999. "School Finance Induced Migration Patterns: The Impact of Private School Vouchers." *Journal of Economic Theory*.

Nechyba, Thomas. "Mobility, Targeting and Private School Vouchers." *American Economic Review* (forthcoming).

Peterson, Paul E., David Myers, Josh Haimson, and William G. Howell. 1997. "Initial Findings from the Evaluation of the New York School Choice Scholarships Program." Mathematica Policy Research. Internet at http://hdc-www.harvard.edu/pepg/index.htm.

Peterson, Paul E., William G. Howell, and Jay P. Greene. 1998. "An Evaluation of the Cleveland Voucher Program After Two Years." Working Paper, Harvard Program on Education Policy and Governance. Internet at http://hdc-www.harvard.edu/pepg/index.htm.

Peterson, Paul E., David Myers, and William G. Howell. 1999. "An Evaluation of the Horizon Scholarship Program in the Edgewood Independent School District, San Antonio, Texas: The First Year." Working Paper, Harvard Program on Education Policy and Governance. Internet at http://hdc-www.harvard.edu/pepg/index.htm.

Peterson, Paul E., David Myers, and William G. Howell. 1998. "An Evaluation of the New York City School Choice Scholarships Program: The First Year." Working Paper, Harvard Program on Education Policy and Governance. Internet at http://hdc-www.harvard.edu/pepg/index.htm.

Rouse, Cecilia Elena. 1998. "Private School Vouchers and Student Achievement: An Evaluation of the Milwaukee Parental Choice Program." *The Quarterly Journal of Economics* CXIII (May): 553-602.

Sullivan, John L., James E. Piereson, and George E. Marcus. 1982. *Political Tolerance and American Democracy*. Chicago: University of Chicago Press.

US Department of Education. 1997. "Findings from the Condition of Education 1997: Public and Private Schools: How Do They Differ?" National Center for Education Statistics. Internet at http://nces.ed.gov/pubs97/97983.html.

Williams, Joe. 2000. "Ex-Milwaukee evaluator endorses school choice: Opponents of program have used his earlier work to argue it has failed." *The Milwaukee Journal-Sentinel* (9 January): 1.

Witte, John F. 1999. "The Milwaukee Voucher Experiment." *Educational Evaluation and Policy Analysis* 20 (no. 4, Winter): 236-37.

Wolf, Patrick J., Jay P. Greene, Brett Kleitz, and Kristina Thalhammer. 2000. "Private Schooling and Political Tolerance, Evidence from College Students in Texas." Harvard Program on Education Policy and Governance Conference (March).

Wolf, Patrick J., William G. Howell, and Paul E. Peterson. 2000. "School Choice in Washington, D.C.: An Evaluation After One Year." Working Paper, Harvard Program on Education Policy and Governance. Internet at http://hdc-www.harvard.edu/pepg/index.htm.

Notes

1   There had earlier been a choice experiment in Alum Rock, but it only included public schools and was so compromised in its implementation that it shed virtually no light on the effects of school choice.

2   See for example James S. Coleman, Thomas Hoffer, Sally Kilgore, *High School Achievement*, (New York: Basic Books), 1982; James S. Coleman, Thomas Hoffer, Sally Kilgore, "Questions and Answers: A Response to our Critics," *Harvard Educational Review* 51 (November 1981), pp. 526-45; James S. Coleman, Thomas Hoffer, Sally Kilgore, "Achievement and Segregation in Secondary Schools: A Further Look at Public and Private School Differences," *Sociology of Education* 55 (April/July 1982), pp. 162-83. *The Harvard Educational Review* and *Sociology of Education* issues contained several critical essays and Coleman's responses.

3   See for example, Henry M. Levin, "Educational Vouchers: Effectiveness, Choice, and Costs," *Journal of Policy Analysis and Management*, vol. 17, no. 3, Summer 1998; Amy Stuart Welles, *A Time to Choose* (New York: Hill and Wang), 1993; and Peter W. Cookson, School Choice: A Struggle for the Soul of American Education (New Haven: Yale Press), 1994.

4   Paul E. Peterson, William G. Howell, and Jay P. Greene, "An Evaluation of the Cleveland Voucher Program After Two Years," Harvard Program on Education Policy and Governance Working Paper, 1998, available at http://hdc-www. harvard.edu/pepg/index.htm ; See also Jay P. Greene, William G. Howell, and Paul E. Peterson, "Lessons from the Cleveland Scholarship Program," *Learning From School Choice* (Washington, D.C.: Brookings Press), 1998.

5   Paul E. Peterson, Jay P. Greene, William G. Howell and William McCready, "Initial Findings from an Evaluation of School Choice Programs in Washington, D.C. and Dayton, Ohio," Harvard Program on Education Policy and Governance Working Paper, 1998; Paul E. Peterson, David Myers and William G. Howell, "An Evaluation of the New York City: School Choice Scholarships Program: The First Year," Harvard Program on Education Policy and Governance Working Paper, 1998; and Paul E. Peterson, David Myers and William G. Howell, "An Evaluation of the Horizon Scholarship Program in the Edgewood
     Independent School District, San Antonio, Texas: The First Year," Harvard Program on Education Policy and Governance Working Paper, 1999. All of these papers are available at http://hdc-www.harvard.edu/pepg/index.htm .

6   Jay P. Greene, Paul E. Peterson, and Jiangtao Du, "School Choice in Milwaukee: A Randomized Experiment," *Learning From School Choice* (Washington, D.C.: Brookings Press), 1998, p. 345. See also Jay P. Greene, Paul E. Peterson, and Jiangtao Du, "Effectiveness of School Choice: The Milwaukee Experiment," *Education and Urban Society*, vol. 31, no. 2, February, 1999.

7   These changes in standard deviation are calculated using the variance in the national sample of the Iowa Test of Basic Skills not the variance in the sample examined in Milwaukee. The standard deviation gains would be even larger if we used the Milwaukee sample as the basis of comparison.

8   Jay P. Greene, Paul E. Peterson, and Jiangtao Du, "School Choice in Milwaukee: A Randomized Experiment," *Learning From School Choice* (Washington, D.C.:

Brookings Press), 1998, p. 344. They did, however, differ significantly on their educational expectations, but it is not clear that this was information collected before participation in the choice program.

9 Jay P. Greene, Paul E. Peterson, and Jiangtao Du, "School Choice in Milwaukee: A Randomized Experiment," *Learning From School Choice* (Washington, D.C.: Brookings Press), 1998, p. 349. The fact that the benefit does not appear to decline when students who are not in private schools are included in the treatment group suggests that the benefit results from being offered a choice to find a suitable school for each child. For some students that suitable choice may be a private school and for some that suitable choice may be a public school.

10 Paul E. Peterson, William G. Howell, and Jay P. Greene, "An Evaluation of the Cleveland Voucher Program After Two Years," Harvard Program on Education Policy and Governance Working Paper, 1998, Table 12, available at http://hdc-www.harvard.edu/pepg/index.htm ; See also Jay P. Greene, William G. Howell, and Paul E. Peterson, "Lessons from the Cleveland Scholarship Program," *Learning From School Choice* (Washington, D.C.: Brookings Press), 1998.

11 An internal school district report from the small school choice program in Florida shows the same lack of differences in the test scores of departing and remaining students.

12 It is also true that there are fewer choice students with physical or learning disabilities. In part this may be explained by the differential labeling and segregating of disabled students in public and private schools. In part this may also be explained by the fact that the cost of educating some disabled students far exceeds the amount provided by the scholarship or voucher. It would be interesting to see whether private schools might take on many more disabled students if they were provided with even some of the additional funding that public schools receive for educating those students.

13 See Gary Burtless, ed., Does Money Matter, (Washington, D.C.: Brookings Press), 1996.

14 In actuality, the development of the public school system was driven to a large degree by fears of Catholic immigrants and the values they would teach their children. This anti-Catholic origin of public schooling has remarkably been replaced with strong myths about the egalitarian and tolerant qualities of public education. See Charles Leslie Glenn, Jr., *The Myth of the Common School* (Amherst, University of Massachusetts Press) 1988.

15 See for example, Hellen Ladd and Edward Fiske, *School Choice in New Zealand: A Cautionary Tale* (Washington, D.C.: Brookings) 2000; Amy Stuart Welles, "Why Some Win and Others Lose in the Educational Marketplace," and J. Douglas Willms and Frank H. Echols, "The Scottish Experience of Parental School Choice," in Edith Rassell and Richard Rothstein, eds, *School Choice: Examining the Evidence* (Washington, D.C.: Economic Policy Institute) 1993.

16 See Amy Gutmann, *Democratic Education* (Princeton: Princeton University Press) 1987; Stephen Macedo, *Diversity and Distrust*, Cambridge: Harvard University Press) 2000; and Benjamin Barber, "Education for Democracy," *The Good Society* 7 (Spring 1997).

17 The privately funded scholarships pay less than $2,000 per pupil while on average public schools spend $6,624, almost three times in constant dollars what

was spent three decades ago. (http://nces.ed.gov/fastfacts/display.asp?id=66) The program in Cleveland pays a little more than $2,000 and the program in Milwaukee pays about half of the per pupil expenditure in Milwaukee public schools. Of course, private schools sometimes receive subsidies from sponsoring religious organizations, but this generally constitutes no more than a few hundred dollars per pupil. And public schools spend some of their money on transportation and special education services, but these do not account for the entirety of the difference between public and private school expenditures. It is also worth remembering that private schools often educate special education students, but they may not always label and segregate those students, allowing for an isolation of those costs.

An Evaluation of New Zealand's Targeted Individual Entitlement Scheme

MICHAEL GAFFNEY AND ANNE B. SMITH
Children's Issues Centre, University of Otago,
Dunedin, New Zealand

Background

New Zealand's Targeted Individual Entitlement (TIE) scheme was established in 1996 to enable children from low-income families to access private education. Families whose taxable household income is less than NZ $25,000 per annum (approximately $16,000 Canadian[1]) and who are not asset rich[2] are eligible for this voucher program. The Ministry of Education pays the participating private schools 110 percent of the national average cost of education for each TIE student they take[3] and pays the families an allowance of between NZ $900 and NZ $1100 to cover non-tuition expenses. TIE was introduced as a pilot scheme for three years in 1996, and after being studied by the authors and deemed successful by the government, was given funding in 1998 to continue indefinitely.

The scheme is a targeted choice scheme, as it provides support specifically for students from low-income families who would normally attend state schools. The TIE scheme gave explicit direction to schools that the selection should give all students an equal chance of being selected, rather than being targeted at academically able students. It offers an all-or-nothing entitlement and does not involve sliding scales of entitlement according to family income. A new scheme called Maori[4] Enhanced Targeted Individual Entitlement—Whakapiki Tauira—was started in 2000 and will be described at the end of this chapter.

The TIE scheme was designed to extend parental choice into the private sector and has produced much debate about the privatization of education and the desirability (or otherwise) of alternative funding schemes such as voucher systems. The state remains the main provider of education in New Zealand. Schools in New Zealand are either described as state, state integrated,[5] or private (independent).[6]

The TIE scheme, therefore, stands as a trial of an alternative form of state-funded education, albeit on a very small scale. It provides the opportunity for a small number of students to choose a school they would not otherwise have had the opportunity to attend by creating entitlements to education funding that can be transferred from the state sector to the private sector. It is a small project alongside the other reforms within the state system of education in New Zealand that have been characterized by 3 features: parental choice, per-student funding formulae, and self-managing schools (Wylie 1999).

The scheme is similar to other schemes adopted elsewhere, such as the Assisted Places Scheme (APS) in England, or the Milwaukee private-school choice experiment in the U.S.A. All three schemes used public funding to make private schooling available to students from low-income families. These schemes are often described as voucher schemes.

This study looks at how successful the TIE scheme has been from the perspective of children, parents, school administrators, and teachers, as well as how successful it has been in achieving the government's goals. The results of this study, however, cannot be used directly to support or discredit arguments about the merits or demerits of voucher schemes at the larger system level.[7]

The evaluation of the TIE scheme was conducted over three years, the first three cohorts of families being followed from when they joined the scheme until the end of 1998 (or their exit from the scheme). Questions were addressed to participating schools, parents, and students. For schools, the focus was on their satisfaction with the scheme and on the progress of the children, any problems and how they might be addressed, and how the process of selecting students was carried out. For parents, the focus was on the background of the families, on the scheme's success at providing parental choice, and on their child's progress. For children, the focus was on their adjustment to and satisfaction with their school. Three reports (Smith & Gaffney 1997; Gaffney & Smith 1998; Gaffney & Smith 1999) give detailed results of each year of the evaluation. This chapter gives an overview of the findings.

Research Questions

The study sought to answer the following questions:[8]
 (I) Selection and Recruitment: Is the TIE scheme successful in re-
     cruiting and selecting the group of students that the Ministry is
     attempting to target?
 (II) Schools—Satisfaction, Problems, Resources: To what extent are
     schools satisfied with the success of the scheme from their point
     of view and from the point of view of the child's progress?
(III) Families—Characteristics, Satisfaction, Problems: What sort of
     families participated in the scheme and how satisfied are they with
     their child's progress? If there were problems what were they?
(IV) Child Well-being: How do children perceive their school situation?

Results   The results are summarized under four headings across each
of the three years of data.[9]

(I) Selection and Recruitment of Families

This section describes the families who joined the scheme and then
looks at the wider group of applicants and who was successful in gaining a place in the scheme.

The families selected into the scheme were often single parents,
reasonably well educated and from a range of socio-economic backgrounds. Half were of New Zealand European (Pakeha) ethnicity and
the other half consisted of Maori, Asian, and European-born parents.
There was a very large proportion of single parents (nearly two-thirds
compared to a quarter in the general population) among the TIE families. The median income for participating families was $15-20,000 com-
pared to the 1996 Census median income for two-parent families with
dependent children of $45,900 and for single-parent families with de-
pendent children of $14,300.

Families who participated in the TIE scheme were generally better
educated at the secondary school level than the general population, as
shown in Figure 1, but they were not more likely to have been to a
private school than the general population.

The scheme was greatly over-subscribed with many more families
making applications than there were places available. There were 604
applications for 1997, 524 for 1998, and 415 applications for 1999. Half

Figure 1   Highest Secondary School Qualifications of Parents and Caregivers

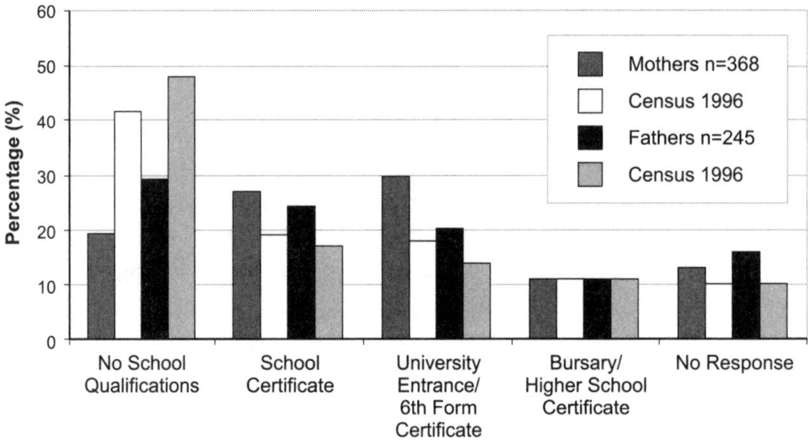

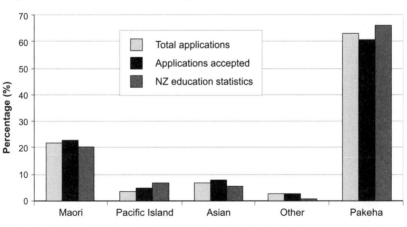

the TIE students were accepted at the elementary level and half at the secondary level, which was the intention of the scheme.

Overall the scheme was successful in recruiting Maori and Asian students relative to other groups, since they were better represented amongst TIE families than in the education statistics (Ministry of Education 1998, p. 4) (See Figure 2). New Zealand European (Pakeha) and

Figure 2   Ethnicity of student applicants

Pacific Island students participated less than the statistics predicted. Figure 2 shows the percentage of applicants across the total number of applications made and places accepted.

(II) Schools

Participating schools were as diverse as the TIE students they accepted. Of the 51 schools that had TIE scheme students in 1998, 23 were elementary, 11 were secondary, and 17 composite (years 1-13). Of these same schools 12 were boys only, 10 were girls only, and 29 were co-educational. Table 1 provides some other background information about TIE scheme schools. There was quite a variation in enrolment size and number of teachers. Just over half of the schools had rolls within the 25 to 300 range. Some schools offered a number of students full-fee scholarships that might be equivalent to TIE scheme places, while many others offered a number of partial-fee scholarships.

It is difficult to characterize the schools when they reflect a diverse range of approaches to education. However, when principals were asked why their school participated in the TIE scheme a large majority, three quarters, said it was to help poor children benefit from private schooling or whatever it was that defined the school as different from state schools. For some schools that was a Christian education or a particular approach to curriculum.

The Independent Schools Council (ISC) was responsible for allocating a number of TIE places from the pool of 160 available each year

Table 1 Some Characteristics of School Sample (n=45)

Characteristics (number of responses)	Mean	SD	Minimum	Maximum
Roll size (51 – based on Ministry of Ed 1997 Stats)[10]	377.1	312.3	27	1346
Number of teachers (42)	27.1	23.4	2	94
Percent of income from fees[11] (34)	82.7	18.1	20	100
Number of part fee paying scholarships (36)	10.3	16.2	0	84
Number of full fee paying scholarships (39)	2.6	4.6	0	24

to interested private schools. The main criterion for schools was that they teach the New Zealand state-school curriculum. Schools would make a request to the ISC for a number of places, according to which they would be allocated a number of places, usually from 1 to 15. The median allocation was between two to four over the period of the trial.

About half of the principals commented that they were restricted in the number of places they could offer because of the demand from fee-paying students. The number of applications schools received over the trial tended to decrease, from a median high of 15 in the first year to a median of 8 applications for the 1999 year. For small schools with class size restrictions, matching applications to the year levels where places were available was difficult.

School Satisfaction

Despite minor reservations, the majority of principals and teachers were very positive about the success of the TIE scheme. They felt that the scheme provided excellent opportunities for the educational success and personal development of the students, and more choice for families on low incomes. In a small number of cases principals identified real benefits for the school as well as for students because the students had contributed so much to the schools.

Both principals and teachers were very positive about the progress of the TIE scheme students within their schools, with principals tending to be even more enthusiastic than teachers. There was support from some principals for the view that the scheme had broadened the cultural and socio-economic base of the school. Most principals and teachers thought that the scheme had benefits for the TIE students, and half thought that there were benefits for the fee-paying students as well.

There was near full agreement from principals and teachers that the scheme should continue at its present level both across the country and at their own school. Indeed they were very happy to expand the scheme so that a larger cohort could begin each year, but few principals felt that their own school would be able to take more students.

Principals and teachers generally thought that TIE scheme students were happy and fitted into their schools very well. They found the students' academic progress and extra-curricular involvement to be similar to, if not better than, other students at the school. This assessment was based on principals' and teachers' perceptions recorded on a rating scale as opposed to the systematic collection of student assessment data.[12] Parents also held this perception that children were progressing well.

The problems associated with the TIE scheme were financial pressure on the families and the schools, especially restrictions on the full participation of students in extracurricular activities because of lack of income. There were also a few cases of social problems for students from low-income families in schools where other students were economically advantaged. There was a strong feeling among principals that the income eligibility criteria for participation in the scheme needed to be revised upwards. There was also some discomfort about the situation for siblings, since only one child per family could participate in the scheme, which was considered unfair. Principals also felt that funding in general should be increased to the families and/or the schools. A few schools suggested different advertising strategies for the program.

Each year a number of TIE scheme students left the scheme because they had either completed their schooling or withdrawn. Eleven per cent of the first and second cohort and one per cent of the third cohort withdrew from the program. Withdrawals occurred for many reasons, including families leaving the locality, health reasons, or difficulties outside or inside the school. Outside difficulties may refer to difficulties with travelling to school or negative attitudes from those outside the school. Internal difficulties included financial pressures, such as the cost of participating in school activities, and social harassment.

Most schools reported that there was a cost to participating in the scheme in forgone revenue. This is because the TIE scheme entitlement received by schools was in most cases less than fees paid by fee-paying families. For elementary year level places (years 1-8) this works out to a median cost to a school of NZ $1,585 per student and at the secondary level (years 9-13) a median cost to a school of NZ $2,500 per student for the 1998 year. This cost to schools assumes all TIE scheme places would have been filled with full-fee paying students. Schools receive 110 percent of the average cost of educating a student in a state school. The extra 10 percent reflects the extra funding low-decile schools[13] receive based on the socio-economic status of their students. Private schools receive a government grant per pupil of about 20 to 40 percent of what state schools receive.

Over the years of the trial, government subsidies to private schools have increased, especially at the secondary level. Private schools now

Table 2 Number of TIE scheme students attending each TIE School

Number of TIE students	Number of schools
0	3[14]
1-5	25
6-10	10
11-15	9
16-20	4
21-25	1
26-30	2
Total	**54**

receive up to 40 percent of what a state school receives for senior secondary school students. So over time the schools have been receiving an increasing ratio of government subsidy for fee-paying students against the amount they receive when taking a TIE scheme student. The schools are aware of the financial costs that they incur from accepting TIE scheme students, and some set a limit of how much money they will forgo and therefore how many TIE scheme students they will take.

Publicity and Recruitment

Over the three years of the study, about half of the schools reported that publicity for the TIE scheme had been sufficient to generate enough applications. Over time fewer of the schools advertised themselves (68 percent in 1996 down to 43 percent in 1998), which seemed to result from their wish not to generate too many applications for the small number of TIE places they had been allocated. They felt that this created disappointment for families who did not get a place. Schools that did not use criteria-based selection for fee-paying students disliked having to find criteria to select TIE scheme students. It seems likely that the number of applications to the program would have been considerably greater if it had been publicized more widely.

Over the years, schools have only slowly increased the number of TIE students on their rolls because of limitations in the schools' capacity. The explanation for this slow increase is partly space restrictions, but finance was also a major factor. The majority of schools reported that they lost income by providing a TIE scheme place, when a fee-paying student could fill it. Two thirds of the schools said there was a limit to the number of TIE students they could take (median 13, range 1 to 50).

1999 was the first year of the scheme when it had not been possible to fill all 160 places from the 415 applications. 149 places were accepted but three applicants withdrew over the summer school holidays, leaving 146 students beginning the scheme in 1999. There are a number of reasons, beyond school capacity constraints, why not all places were filled. For example, there were fewer schools to choose from because at least five of the private schools integrated in the previous year. In 1997 there were 604 applications and in 1998 there were 524. So in 1999 there were fewer applications to draw on. There were also changes to the application process so that there was less time to make sure students filled all available places. The application process for families begins in early August, and families know by early September if they have been successful, with confirmation of acceptance (upon assessment of household income) in early October, four months before the school year starts. In previous years, unfilled places were reallocated right up until the beginning of the school year at the end of January.

(III) Families' Satisfaction with the Scheme

Families generally had very positive perceptions of the TIE scheme and most parents and children agreed that the children were happy, doing well academically, and participating in extracurricular activities. About half of the families coped financially with the extra costs of attending a private school, but 40 percent had serious financial difficulties. Causes of dissatisfaction related to issues such as access for siblings to the scheme and recent changes to the administration of the scheme, such as the later delivery of the allowance to families.

TIE families usually had little choice of private schools. The small number of schools in the scheme meant that only about a fifth of families had more than one private school to choose from. For many families choice was constrained because there was only one suitable school (to match the age and gender of the student) within reasonable travelling distance, and many of the schools were offering places at specific levels. Some schools specified only a single year level for the TIE scheme place or places they were offering.

Reasons for Applying

When the families were asked why they joined the scheme, about half of them referred to the TIE scheme as an opportunity to get a better education. Just under a fifth of families said they had always wanted to send their child to the particular school and that the TIE scheme presented an opportunity to do this. Some of the reasons given to account for this preference were that they wanted their child to go to a single sex school or a school that would support Christian beliefs similar to their own.

When contrasting their private school with the state school their child would have attended, families consistently referred to smaller classes (40 percent); individual attention and discipline (both 25 percent); better teachers and teaching (20 percent); and better resources (10 percent) as reasons for preferring their private school. When asked if there were any reasons for avoiding the state school their child would have most likely attended, the most common reason was that they did not like the school's social environment (25 percent). Twenty percent had no particular reason, and 10 percent wanted to avoid the type of students attending state schools.

Family Satisfaction

Over 90 percent of TIE families were satisfied with the educational and social progress that their children were making. The benefits most likely to be mentioned were improved confidence, self-esteem and maturity; higher achievement and motivation to succeed, and greater participation in extracurricular activities. Over a third of families reported no problems from participating in the scheme. The problems that were reported included increased workload for the children (10 percent), the child's poorer economic resources (compared to other students) (10 percent), and the negative attitudes of students and teachers at the new school (5 percent).

Most families were very positive about their child's private school, and over time this satisfaction was maintained. Parents and caregivers were asked to comment on the types of activities and resources available, how well their child was getting on with others in the school, the amount of work, and the ease of changing schools. In comparison with their child's previous school, the parents rated the private schools very positively on most criteria. Schools were rated as similar to the previous state school on how well the children got on with other students.

The only feature parents perceived as worse was the difficulty in getting to school each day, which reflects the likelihood of travelling much longer distances to a private school.

Families were given an allowance to cover extra costs such as travel, uniforms, and participation in school activities. Families were provided NZ $900 if their child was at the year 1-8 level of school (elementary) and NZ $1,100 if at the year levels 9-13 (secondary). About 50 percent of the families from the first two cohorts reported that the allowance was adequate to cover their extra costs. This was an improvement on their first year when the initial cost of uniforms was a major consideration. About 40 percent of the families reported that the allowance was inadequate in 1998 and that they were carrying a debt over from the previous year[15] in the scheme.

There was provision in the scheme for schools to charge families the difference between what the Ministry of Education entitlement covered and the school fees. Only two schools adopted this practice. This practice of charging TIE families the difference in tuition fees led to two withdrawals from one of the schools. In general, however, schools have shown themselves to be very flexible in finding a solution when families inform them of financial problems. Only two students have ever withdrawn from the scheme because of financial difficulties.

One major issue families raised over the last two years of the scheme was the criteria that only one child from each family could participate in the scheme at any one time. In the first year of the scheme this criteria was not used, and eight sets of siblings were able to join, seven families with two children and one with three. While restricting families to only one child increases the number of families who can participate, the families and schools do not favour this approach. Many of the schools see themselves as working with families rather than individual children and have an expectation that all children from a family will participate in a school. This restriction also creates tensions for the families who must decide if it will be fair to send one child to a private school and not another. For families with multiple children who take on the challenge of joining the scheme, this policy increases the number of schools and systems they have to deal with, and creates complex family travel arrangements. This is a bigger issue for elementary aged children because they are more dependent, and their schooling requires a lot more input from parents and caregivers.

Aside from these minor issues, the majority of parents and caregivers of TIE children judged the TIE scheme very successful.

(IV) Student Well-being

A large majority of TIE students were happy with the program and glad to be attending their new school. Students cited friends, good relationships with students and teachers, and academic achievement as their reasons for their high level of satisfaction with the TIE scheme. On those occasions when things were not going well for students, they referred to the same aspects: not having friends, getting on badly with classmates or teachers, or lack of achievement at school.

Overall the students were very positive about their new schools in terms of: facilities, resources and activities, their teachers, and the other students. Though they were less positive about the level and amount of work required in the new school, most students felt that the level of work was better than at their previous school. Children rated the following features of their new school as much better than their previous school: resources and activities, getting on with other students, and helpfulness of the teachers. Like their parents, their only real criticism was that some found it harder to get to school. In general, while both parents and children were very positive about the TIE schools, the parents were more positive than the students.

There was general agreement among principals, teachers, and parents that the students were doing very well academically, fitting in well socially into their new schools and participating well in extracurricular activities. Principals, teachers, and parents all agreed that students were happy. Students also generally reported that they were happy. We received five times more comments about aspects that made students happy at their private school than aspects that made them unhappy. The most cited reasons for satisfaction were achieving well at school (25 percent), having friends (22 percent), and getting on well with students (39 percent) and teachers (18 percent). These were the same aspects that caused unhappiness at school, i.e., not having friends (3 percent), getting on badly with classmates (16 percent) or teachers (5 percent), or lack of achievement at school (5 percent).

Student enjoyment of school centred on participating in favourite classes and sports activities, having the support of teachers, and a generally positive social environment at school. Students mentioned disliking difficulties they experienced with other students, the amount of work, and the hours of schooling (which for some was exacerbated by travel requirements). Overall, student satisfaction and well-being were favourable.

Conclusions

The findings indicate that the scheme was successful in facilitating access to private schooling for a small number of low-income New Zealand families.

The families who participated in the scheme tended to be headed by a single parent, relatively well-educated, of low income and middle socio-economic status. The TIE families included a similar percentage of Maori to the general population so targeting of Maori children was successful. The scheme was also successful in facilitating access for students from ethnically diverse families.

Both parents and students were highly satisfied with the TIE scheme. Most felt that their children were better off educationally in the private school than in their previous state school. While the number of schools that families could apply to was limited, it did allow this small group of families to choose schools outside of the state system. The reported satisfaction with the scheme was much stronger than any problems with it.

The schools, too, were highly supportive of the scheme, and the TIE students were perceived to have progressed as well as or better than fee-paying students. The schools perceived the scheme to be very beneficial to the students and families. They supported the growth and continuation of the scheme despite concerns over the loss of income the school incurred as a result. While schools would have liked to see the scheme expand, very few thought that their own school could take many more TIE students. Because a relatively large number of private schools integrated into the state system in 1998, the capacity of private schools to absorb more TIE students is limited.

As a result of the preliminary findings of this research the government deemed the TIE scheme a success and decided to continue funding it indefinitely. A change in government at the end of 1999 saw no new students enter the scheme after the year 2000.

The Maori TIE Scheme

In 1998, it was announced that a new scheme would be set up for the indigenous people of New Zealand, the Maori. It is called the Maori Enhanced Targeted Individual Entitlement—Whakapiki Tauira. As a group, Maori students are underachieving in the New Zealand education system, and one of the Ministry's main goals throughout the nineties has been to look for ways to address this achievement gap. Participants in the Maori TIE scheme must have a household income of less than $25,000 and must identify themselves as Maori. The money provided need not be used in a private school, and the purposes for which it can be used were unspecified. The selection of students for this scheme was centralized, not done through the schools themselves. Another major difference between this scheme and the original TIE scheme was that the money provided was added to what the schools already received for educating these students.

Applications were made available in places frequented by Maori families who might benefit from the scheme. The Ministry of Education received 3,400 applications for the 130 places available. This was four to five times the number that the TIE scheme received each year. Indeed, there seemed to be a separate group of families wanting the Maori TIE as opposed to the earlier TIE scheme option. Only 12 of the applications were for private schools and none of these were successful.

It was left open-ended as to how families could use the funds, but it was suggested that funds might cover school fees, travel, after-school activities, and information technology. The main criterion for selection was that the students would attend a school with a credible Maori Language and Culture Program. Those families most in need, that is, those students in single-parent families or difficult housing circumstances, were given priority. In addition, attempts were made to improve access to curriculum opportunities, and priority was given to students from rural areas, those likely to have dropped out if they had not been able to change schools, and those who might reach their potential with extra tuition. The selection committee tried to provide the best return on the funds by offering them to students who would use them to change schools.

Of the 130 places given, 88 percent were provided to students attending Maori boarding schools. One hundred twenty-two of these students were going to secondary schools, leaving only 8 at the elementary level. Some changes to the criteria are expected to be made in order to improve the selection process, and some attempt will be made to increase the number of successful elementary applications. Due to a change in government, it is unclear whether the Maori TIE scheme will continue.

References

Gaffney, M. and A.B. Smith. 1999. *Evaluation of the TIE Scheme: Report 3*. Report to the Ministry of Education, Children's Issues Centre.
———. 1998 *Evaluation of the TIE Project: A Second Preliminary Report*. Report 2 to the Ministry of Education, Children's Issues Centre.
Ministry of Education. 1998. "July 1998 School Statistics." *Education Statistics News Sheet*, 8 (11), November. Data Management and Analysis Division.
Smith, A.B., and M. Gaffney. 1997. *Evaluation of the TIE Project: A Preliminary Report*. Report 1 to the Ministry of Education. Children's Issues Centre.
Wylie, C. 1999. "Is the Land of the Flightless Bird the Home of the Voucherless Voucher?" *New Zealand Journal of Educational Studies* 34 (1), 99-109.

Notes

1   At the time of writing the New Zealand dollar was equivalent to approximately 64 cents Canadian.
2   The term asset rich was never defined in the information sent to parents applying to the scheme. Nevertheless, all applicants to the scheme had to sign a form that said "My household has few assets".
3   In 1998 this was NZ $4051 for year 1-6 students, NZ $4496 for year 7-8 students, NZ $6299 for year 9-10 students and NZ $7088 for year 11-13 students with additional allowances being paid to families for uniform and other costs ($900 for elementary and $1100 for secondary students).
4   The term Maori is used to describe the indigenous people of New Zealand.
5   There are 306 state integrated schools in New Zealand. These schools follow the state curriculum requirements, retaining their 'special character' (e.g. religious observances) but with the proprietors providing the accommodation while the state pays day-to-day expenses, including teachers' salaries. This option was brought about by the Private Schools Conditional Integration Act of 1975, which allowed independent schools to gain access to more state funding but at the same time allow them to retain their special character. The Catholic schools in New Zealand came under the state integrated designation in the early 1980's.
6   The July 1998 School Statistics show that enrolments at private schools totalled 24,836, or 3.4 percent of the New Zealand school population. That year, 118 of the 2779 schools in New Zealand were independent schools. Just over half of the independent schools are in New Zealand's three largest cities of Auckland, Wellington and Christchurch. The schools in these three areas take just under three quarters (72.6%) of the students enrolled at independent schools in New Zealand.
7   Arguments about alternative funding arrangements such as 'vouchers' have been vigorous. Advocates for such schemes have argued they will: increase parental choice; provide valuable competition between schools and so improve quality; allow parents to exit from inferior schools; get rid of the monopoly of

state education and increase equity because of increased choice for poor families; promote parent affiliation to schools; and reduce administration costs. Opponents have criticized them as an attack on state schools because of the negative impact on state schools (which may run down and lose critical mass); the loss of a public agenda for education (e.g. cultural or civic values); lack of equity of access and easier access for families with cultural capital; the need for bureaucracy and regulation; and accentuating individualistic and meritocratic ideals rather than social cohesion.

8　A Postal Survey with separate questionnaires designed for principals, teachers, parents and year 7-13 students was undertaken each year. In order to provide qualitative data more likely to give a richer understanding of the issues for parents, children and schools, and allow issues to be explored in depth, the study included a small sample of schools and families from two areas, who were interviewed face to face. One area was chosen in the first year and the other in the second year of the study. No new interviews were conducted in the final year. Follow-up interviews with participants from the first two cohorts were conducted each year by phone with interviewees. All of the principal and parent interviews took place within the school and most of the student and family interviews took place at home.

9　All three cohorts of families are reported as one group. In the main the cohorts are very similar but any significant differences between the three cohorts will be noted.

10　The numbers in brackets refer to the number of responses to this question. It was, however, possible to get roll size figures for all 51 schools from the Ministry of Education. The July 1997 figures were used from the Ministry of Education (1998) Directory of NZ Schools and Tertiary Institutions, January 1998.

11　This figure does not include the government subsidy.

12　There are no academic assessment tools used by all New Zealand schools except national exams that occur at the end of year 11 & 13. Year 13 is the final year of high school in New Zealand.

13　New Zealand schools are given a ranking from 1 to 10 based on the socioeconomic status of the families that contribute to a particular school. A ranking of 1 reflects a low SES school and 10 a high SES school.

14　These schools have previously had TIE scheme students but currently don't.

15　The debt amounted to an average of $562 for those who were in their second year, and an average of $736 for those who were in their third year. These figures do not include data from the nine per cent of families who had a child boarding, for whom it was never anticipated that the allowance would meet their boarding costs.

Serving the Needs of the Poor: The Private Education Sector in Developing Countries

JAMES TOOLEY, Ph.D.
Professor of Education Policy,
University of Newcastle, England

A Touching Faith

Maris O'Rourke, Director of Education at the World Bank—and previously the Secretary for Education in New Zealand—was asked at a recent conference in London[1] why she thought that governments should be involved in education. "The bottom line," she said, "is to promote equity." There were many murmurs of assent in the room.

My experience is that this is the bottom line for most people who give this matter any thought. Equity—or one of its popular near-synonyms, equality of opportunity or just plain equality—is the principle reason why government intervention in education is justified. There are other reasons, but the promotion of equity seems to be the most intuitively obvious and appealing. This is neatly encapsulated in one recent Canadian anti-privatization book, *No More Teachers, No More Books*, by Heather-Jane Robertson:

> Giving all children the opportunity to enjoy an equal education, determined not by the wealth of their families but by the resources of their communities, is ... a truly democratic ideal ...a shared public commitment in achieving greater equity is *the only reason for public schools to exist.* (Robertson 1998, 188)

I find it a rather touching faith that governments could provide equity in education, given their record to date. As Robertson notes, this is an ideal which "has never been fully realized" (188). But it's touching to think that she, and others like her, suppose that it ever could be realized. In the developed world, we see huge disparity in the quality and standard of state schools from middle-class to working-class areas. For developing countries, a key proxy indicator for inequity is the proportion of public funds spent on primary schools as opposed to higher education. Higher education is the province of a tiny elite, by and large, in developing countries; the poor generally have access only to primary education. Given this fact, we would assume that an equitable system would spend a small proportion of public funding on higher education, to reflect the small number of young people who pass through to university, and the bulk of its funds on primary education. The reality is very different. For example, in the 22 countries in Black Africa, 15 percent of all public expenditure goes to the 2 to 3 percent of the population who are going on to higher education. In Latin America and the Caribbean, the figure is 17 percent (UNESCO Database 1994).

These raw statistics don't convey the true human story behind these figures, though. At a recent United Nations expert group meeting in New York, the economist Larry Willmore told the story of his highly intelligent secretary in Brazil. Larry found that this woman, from a very poor background, was studying for her degree at was widely thought to be an inferior private university and paying expensive fees to boot. Why was she doing this? It was obvious, she said. Yes, she had been accepted to the elitist—and free—public university. But she had to work to support herself and her family, and the public university ran courses only during the day; the private university, aware of its customers' needs, offered classes at night. And she could do her degree in far less time than at the public university. In other words, the public university was specifically geared for the children of the upper middle classes, who could afford the leisurely progress of full-time study, supported by generous and long-suffering parents; it was not set up for the less privileged. Yet this, and similar universities around the world, receive a hugely disproportionate amount of public funds.

So, as I say, a touching faith that governments can provide equity in education. Nonetheless, I guess that people like Ms. Robertson would argue that, while governments might not have succeeded perfectly, they would much better achieve equity than any privatized alternative, that is, where the private sector, including philanthropists, agencies of civil society, and commercial organizations take a greater role in education. I've argued at length elsewhere that such an assumption is completely wrong, that the private alternative *can* deliver equity or equality of opportunity and that democratic states cannot, for good solid theoretical reasons (see Tooley 2000a, Session 2). In this chapter, I want to put some flesh on these abstract arguments. Even if it's true in theory, how can it be true in practice? In particular, I want to show how untenable is the common assumption about the private sector in education, that it caters only to the elite, and hence that its promotion is bound only to exacerbate inequality. On the contrary, I suggest that recent research from developing countries points in the opposite direction. If we want to help some of the most disadvantaged peoples in the world, then encouraging deeper private sector involvement is likely to be the best way forward. And if it is true for some of the poorest in the world, I also suspect that it is likely to be true for the less advantaged in developed countries such as Canada, the US, and the UK.

To show this, this paper examines first how public, that is, state, education serves some of the poorest in society and then contrasts this information with findings about private schools. Research that has directly compared the two sectors is also summarized. Brief notes are also made about other innovative ways in which the private education sector is also helping the poor, before these themes are drawn together in the concluding section.

Does Public Education Serve the Needs of the Poor?

To explore what to many will be a counterintuitive proposition, that private education can help the poor, let's begin with investigating the lot of some of the poorest people on the planet, the poor who live in the slums and villages in India. First, how do government schools serve these people? The Indian government recently sponsored the PROBE Report—the *Public Report on Basic Education in India* (The Probe Team, 1999)—which gives a useful picture of the relative merits of public and private schools for the poor.

The relevant parts of the PROBE Report look at primary education in four states—Bihar, Madhya Pradesh, Uttar Pradesh, and Rajasthan. In these four states, the fieldwork surveyed a sample of 188 villages, more or less selected as a random sample from all villages in the 300-3,000 population range.[2] In these 188 villages, there were a total of 195 government schools and 41 private schools. Teachers, parents, and children from all of these schools were interviewed. In all, this came to a total of 1,221 households, 2,820 of 6- to 14-year-old children, 650 government and 186 private school teachers.

The picture that the report paints of the government schools is bleak indeed. It describes the "malfunctioning" in these schools for the poor. The schools suffer from poor physical facilities and high pupil-teacher ratios, but what is most disturbing is the low level of teaching taking place in them. When researchers called unannounced on their random sample of schools, "teaching activity" was going on in only 53 percent of them (47). In fully 33 percent, the headteacher was absent. But even these figures overestimate what was typically taking place, because this report includes only those schools that were actually open when the researchers visited. Moreover, the researchers usually visited in late morning, which was the time of peak school activity. Finally, "teaching activity" is construed broadly to include children reading aloud or being supervised while doing their own written work.

Clearly, poor infrastructure and apathetic parents are a problem; the Indian overly-academic curriculum can be paralyzing to teachers and students alike; teachers are burdened with excessive paperwork, and there is unsupportive and inadequate management. But the deterioration of teaching standards results not just from disempowered teachers:

> The PROBE survey came across many instances where an element of plain negligence was ... involved. These include several cases of irresponsible teachers keeping a school closed or non-functional for months at a time; a school where the teacher was drunk, while only one sixth of the children enrolled were present; other drunk teachers, some of who expect pupils to bring them *daru* [drink]; a headteacher who asks the children to do domestic chores, including looking after the baby; several cases of teachers sleeping at school; ... a headteacher who comes to school once a week; another headteacher who did not know the name of a single child in the school ... (63).

Significantly, the low level of teaching activity occurred even in those schools with relatively good infrastructure, teaching aids, and pupil-teacher ratio. Even in such schools, however,

> Inactive teachers were found engaged in a variety of pastimes such as sipping tea, reading comics, or eating peanuts, when they were

not just sitting idle. Generally, teaching activity has been reduced to a minimum, in terms of both time and effort. And this pattern is not confined to a minority of irresponsible teachers—it has become a way of life in the profession. (63).

But all of these findings highlight, for the PROBE researchers, the underlying problem in the government schools: the "deep lack of accountability in the schooling system" (54).

Is there any alternative but these schools for the poor? Surely no one else can do better than government, given the low level of resources available? Not so. The PROBE report pointed to the existence of many private schools that were serving the same populations and conceded—rather reluctantly, it seems—that such problems were not found in these schools. In the great majority of private schools—again visited unannounced and at random—there "was feverish classroom activity" (102). Private schools, they said, were successful because they were more accountable:

> This feature of private schools brings out the key role of *accountability* in the schooling system. In a private school, the teachers are accountable to the manager (who can fire them), and, through him or her, to the parents (who can withdraw their children). In a government school, the chain of accountability is much weaker, as teachers have a permanent job with salaries and promotions unrelated to performance. This contrast is perceived with crystal clarity by the vast majority of parents. (64).

The report continues: "As parents see it, the main advantage of private schools is that, being more accountable, they have higher levels of teaching activity. This is confirmed by the PROBE survey" (102). Moreover, in interviews with large sample of parents, "Most parents stated that, if the costs of sending a child to a government and private school were the *same*, they would rather send their children to a private school" (102).

Private Schools for the Poor?

To many readers, the existence of such private schools for the poor will be a surprise, so a few details about their structure and organization may be appropriate. I came across such schools in India while conducting fieldwork for the International Finance Corporation, the private finance arm of the World Bank. Officials with whom I was working in India seemed wary of introducing me to any of these schools, although they acknowledged their existence. So I set off alone one day, first by auto-rickshaw, then on foot, into the slum areas behind the Charminar in Hyderabad, the capital of Andhra Pradesh, and there they were, almost at every street corner, down every alley, another private school or col-lege. And, as luck would have it, I found a few schools where the headteachers were welcoming and spoke English, and who were able to introduce me to the loose federation under which many of them worked, the Federation of Private Schools' Management. From then on, I was inundated with principals of schools who wanted to meet me, show me what they were doing, and how they had to cope with severe govern-ment regulations.

In Andhra Pradesh as a whole, private unaided[3] schools make up 11 percent of enrolment in elementary schools, with more than 30 percent at the upper primary level. In addition, there are an estimated 3,000 unrecognized unaided schools, with 80,000 students. The Federation, which was formed in 1997 by a group of unaided private school corre-spondents and principals, has 500 schools in Andhra Pradesh, of which 40 percent are recognized by government, 60 percent are not.

Elsewhere (Tooley 2000b), I have described further details on 13 of these schools for which I gained usable data. Briefly, the facts about these are as follows. Schools ranged in size from 100 students—in a school that had just opened and was seeking to grow—to the largest at 2,000. Pupil fees varied according to the grade level of the child. The lowest fees charged ranged from 25 to 35 rupees per month (about 60 to 83 US cents per month). The highest fees ranged from 150 to 200 rupees per month (about US $3.57 to $4.76 per month). A typical school charged about US $10 to $20 per year.[4]

Even though these schools are for the poor, a key feature is that they have a significant number of scholarships—that is, free places for even poorer students. The free places were allocated by the School Cor-respondent, on the basis of claims of need checked informally in the community. Five of the schools had between 15 and 20 percent of stu-dents in free school places.

The smallest school had three teachers, the largest 70. For all of the schools, the teacher-pupil ratio varied between 1:22 to 1:35. (This is one of the noted features of the private schools, that their teacher-pupil ratio is much lower than in the government schools).

In a state school, the average teacher pay varies between about 4,000 rupees to 9,000 rupees per month (about $95 to $200), depending on qualifications. In these unaided private schools it was significantly lower, from as low as 400 to 600 rupees per month in the rural school (i.e., $9.50 to $14.20 per month) to a high of 2000 to 5000 rupees per month ($47.60 to $119.00) in the city. As for teacher qualifications, all of the schools had teachers qualified at least to the intermediate (grade 12) level, and the great majority of schools had mainly graduate teachers. Some schools had Masters' graduates, and one a Ph.D.

The governing structure for all thirteen of the schools was technically the same. Each was managed by an associated educational, religious, or charitable society, as constituted under the 1860 Act, and as required for the schools to be recognized by the government under the Andhra Pradesh 1982 Education Act. (This, and other regulations stipulate that if a school is to be recognized, it must be such a society and not run for profit). However, it is very important to note that this did not mean that any school was run as a charity, funded by charitable donations. Without exception, all of the schools were run on commercial business principles, in the sense that they were self-financing, gaining all of their funds from student fees, commercial loans, or sales of goods. Most of the schools also appeared to make a small surplus which was, in principle, reinvested in the school.

This said, it was also the case that all of the correspondents and principals interviewed claimed to be motivated by a concern for the poor communities in which they worked. Many described themselves as social workers and clearly derived considerable satisfaction from being willing to help in areas that were not on the face of it particularly promising. Typical comments came from Mr. Mohamed Wajid, Director and Correspondent of Peace High School: "These people belong to a slum area, they totally depend upon us, they totally trust us," he said. His mother had encouraged him to take over the school when she was ready to retire. "She showed me pictures of the poor people living here, and reminded me that life must not be lived for oneself; life must be lived for others. So she made me take over the running of her school."

Given the existence of these private schools and the way they are responding to the needs of the poor, it might be thought that the government was assisting them in their task. In fact, the opposite is true. As one of the principals put it to me: "Sometimes government is the obstacle of the people." At every turn, it would seem that government regulations were getting in the way of the smooth and effective operation of these schools. Indeed, only two out of the 13 schools (15 percent) had full recognition from government. Two major problems arise for parents from their schools not being recognized. First, very importantly, only at government-recognized schools can students sit their school (Grade 7 and 10) examinations. However, the schools in the Federation (and more widely) have found a neat way around this. There is nothing in the statutory regulations to stop unrecognized schools from sending their students to a recognized school as "private candidates" for the purpose of taking examinations. This loophole is used to great effect within the Federation. However, this process costs more for parents. To take an examination in their own school costs 50 rupees per entry (about $1), but as a private candidate, they have to pay five times this, 250 rupees per entry (for some of the schools this is almost equivalent to the annual student fee). This is a major disadvantage for parents.

The second disadvantage is that students have "private" candidate stamped on their certificate, not the name of a school. Not only do some high schools, colleges, and universities look down on this status and prefer candidates from a named—especially a named *known*—school, it also is an inconvenience, as most high schools or colleges will ask for other proof of residence and identity when a student applies for entry, whereas with an ordinary certificate this additional proof is not required.

So why don't the schools get government recognition? The problem is that there are many regulations that make it virtually impossible for many private schools for the poor to do so. Three conditions in particular were described as onerous and difficult to meet:

- To be recognized, the statutory rules state that a school must have a playground of 1000 square yards—clearly beyond the reach of most such poor schools in the slums, given availability and cost of land.
- There is also a requirement for government-trained teachers within the school. But teacher training colleges offer only vernacular-medium teaching certificates for primary schools, but most of the private schools are English-medium. So although there are no state offered qualifications for teachers to take, the government refuses to recognize schools which do not have state-qualified teachers: catch 22!
- To be recognized, the society must deposit a "corpus" or endowment fund of 25,000 rupees or 50,000 rupees (depending on the level of school, i.e., up to $1,200) in a stipulated bank account. In itself, this is extremely hard to find for many schools. I estimate that for at least seven of the schools this was greater than their annual surplus!

In summary, what the PROBE report shows is that

1. Poor parents are willing to pay for their children to attend unaided private schools because they perceive the quality of the private schools to be higher than in government schools.
2. The quality *is* (in fact, not only in perception) higher in the private schools in terms of:
   • Level of teaching activity and time spent teaching.
   • Commitment and dedication of teachers, resulting in higher levels of teacher activity and closer attention to students.
3. The quality of education is higher because of the accountability of private schools to parents.

But can we say any more about the quality and also the cost-effectiveness of these private schools? Does the increased level of teaching activity and teacher commitment have any impact on the academic and other educational achievements in the private schools? There is quite a bit of other research from developing countries which explores these issues in the more general context of public versus private schools.

Public versus Private Schools in Developing Countries

First, there is the important work by World Bank economist Emmanuel Jimenez and sociologist Marlaine E. Lockheed, and other colleagues who studied "The Relative Efficiency of Private and Public Schools" in Thailand (Jimenez et al. 1991, 205-218; Jimenez et al. 1988, 139-164). The researchers conducted detailed quantitative analysis using longitudinal data and looked for the value added by the school, whether private or public. Using advanced statistical techniques to control for potential bias from social background, the researchers concluded that the private schools are, in general, "more effective and less costly" than their public counterparts at improving the mathematical performance of students. Taking their methods on to a broader canvas, the researchers showed that, based on studies comparing private and public education in Colombia, the Dominican Republic, the Philippines, Tanzania, and Thailand, and focusing now on mathematics and language teaching, private school students again, in general, outperformed the public school students. This result, again, held true even when controlling for the potential bias of social class. And again, there was "preliminary evidence" to suggest that the unit costs in private schools were lower than in the public schools (Jimenez et al. 1991, 205).

In terms of higher education, World Bank economist Estelle James (1991, 189-206) shows that in the Philippines (where 80 percent of all college and university students attend private institutions) the private sector again "operates at much lower cost ... per student than does the public sector," and there is some suggestive evidence to show that this lower cost comes along with higher quality and efficiency. And in terms of public and private schools operating under a state-funded voucher, the evidence from Chile is unequivocal. Chile brought in a system of vouchers in 1980, which allowed for these subsidies to be spent at private schools or at local municipal schools. The evidence shows that the subsidized private schools were more efficient than the municipal schools—employing less teachers per pupil and having lower unit costs. Yet they achieved higher test results in mathematics and Spanish. This result holds even when the test scores are adjusted to control for socio-economic status (Larrañaga 1997).

Finally, there is further evidence from India, which gives an insight into schools closely related to the examples given above. Geeta Kingdon's fascinating work (1996a, b) explores in more detail the question, "Is the popularity of private fee-charging schools in India to be explained by their superior quality?" To explore this question, she constructed a stratified random sample of three types of schools: private-unaided (PUA), private-aided (PA), and government (G) schools, in urban Lucknow, in the state of Uttar Pradesh. The private-aided schools are virtually indistinguishable from government schools. They get a block grant for more or less all of their income, irrespective of student numbers or performance. They are also subject to severe teacher unionization and government regulation. The private-unaided schools are the only category worth considering as genuine private schools.

Kingdon collected data from 902 students of class 8 students (13 to 14-years-old), in 30 schools across the three sectors, on:

- Student achievement measured using adaptations of standardized tests of numeracy and literacy
- Ability of students measured using Ravens Progressive Matrices
- Details of personal, parental, and household characteristics of students
- School income and expenses, teaching materials, and facilities

In order to control for social and personal factors, Kingdon's method was to seek to predict the score for a student with the average charac-

Table 1 Comparison of Achievement Among Government, Private-aided and Private-unaided Schools

		G	PA	PUA
Maths	Raw	8.97	8.36	17.09
	Standardized	11.38	10.09	12.80
Reading	Raw	9.77	10.86	16.85
	Standardized	13.78	13.73	13.83

teristics of a public school pupil if she were to attend a private school, and vice versa. This predicted score was then compared with the actual public school average achievement figure. Table 1 gives these results.

On the raw scores, the private-unaided students scored almost twice as highly as the government and private-aided schools, in both mathematics and reading. However, when these figures were corrected to take into account personal endowments and selectivity of pupils, this superiority decreased somewhat, although it was still statistically significant. For instance, the private-unaided schools, after correction, are still 27 percent more effective at teaching maths than the other schools. However, Kingdon also investigated the cost-effectiveness of the schools, and the findings here are most revealing. Combining the results of standardized achievement in mathematics and language with per pupil expenditures gives the results in Table 2.

Table 2 Comparison of Cost Per Achievement Point in Government, Private-aided and Private-unaided Schools

	G	PA	PUA
Cost per student (Rs)	2008	1827	999
Predicted math score	11.38	10.09	12.80
Cost per math point	176	181	78
Predicted reading score	13.78	13.73	13.82
Cost per reading point	146	133	72
Predicted total score	25.16	23.82	26.62
Cost per achievement point	80	77	38

As before, the predicted total scores are higher in the private-unaided schools. But the costs per student are substantially lower—less than half the costs of the government schools. This means that the "cost per achievement point" in the private-unaided schools is less than half that in the government schools (38 as compared to 80). This is a dramatic result. In other words, private-unaided schools are not only better than government and government-aided schools in terms of student scores, but they are much, much cheaper too.

Of course, education is more than scores in maths and science. Coupled with the evidence from the PROBE report in terms of teacher attention and dedication in schools for the poor, this additional evidence would seem to suggest a very strong case could be made that the private schools in India are much better at serving their clients than government schools, and that is as true for schools for the poor as for any other schools.

Objections to Private Education for the Poor

Perhaps surprisingly, given the positive picture painted of the private sector vis-à-vis the government sector, the PROBE team balked at recommending a greater role for it in primary and secondary schooling. It is worth exploring their reasons, for they may also be the sort of objections to which other anti-privatization people such as Heather-Jane Robertson, noted above, may be sympathetic.

The PROBE team admits that their report has painted a "relatively rosy" picture of the private sector, where "accountability to the parents" leads to "a high level of classroom activity ... better utilization of facilities, greater attention to young children, responsiveness of teachers to parental complaints" (105). But there are four reasons why such findings do not convince them that a greater role for the private sector is desirable or required:

1. Private schools are out of reach for the vast majority of poor parents.
2. Private schools "often take advantage of the vulnerability of parents." This is because many "parents have little idea of what goes on in the classroom. They know that teachers turn up on time, keep the children busy, and maintain discipline, and in all these respects private schools strike them as superior to government schools. Even an inept teacher, however, can maintain these appearances without imparting much education to the children" (105).

3. Private teachers will teach to the test. They have "little reason to promote the personal development of the children, to treat them with sensitivity, or to impart a sense of values. Their overwhelming objective is to cram the heads of the pupils, so that they may pass the relevant tests and examinations" (105).
4. The expansion of private schools will undermine state education: "This carries a real danger of undermining the government schooling system ... [which] may lead to a very divisive pattern of schooling opportunities, with better-off parents sending their children to private schools while poorer parents are left to cope with nonfunctional government schools" (106).

The second and third of these are criticisms of the quality of private education. They are not based on the evidence in their report and would require further research to substantiate. However, my own research (Tooley 2000b) suggests that the quality of private schools for the poor is likely to be much higher than is claimed here. And if one is genuinely concerned with helping the poor, then ways need to be explored which can help these schools to improve—perhaps through helping in capacity-building for teacher training, improving curriculum and pedagogy, quality control, and improved resources.[5] In any case, the Report notes that the problem of teaching-to-the-test "applies in government schools too," but counters this by suggesting that "at least in the latter case there is a possibility of stimulating the interest of teachers in alternative teaching principles and practices." Again, my own research (Tooley 1999) suggests the opposite, that it is in the private schools that the most interest in innovative teaching methods will arise, not in government schools.

The fourth objection is not an objection to private education per se, but to the impact that private education will have on the state system. But if, as the authors report, state education is so bad and private schools are so much better, then why do the authors worry about the demise of state education?, As long as poor parents are not deprived of educational opportunities for their children, why should they object to better schools taking over from worse ones?

Finally, the first objection is well-taken: not all children can afford the private schools. But if the state sector provides schools which are so cavalier about their clients, indifferent to their needs, then this suggests that reformers' efforts would best be served by helping such children attend private schools—whether through public or private voucher/

scholarship schemes (or both)—rather than by objecting to the private sector.

Other Private Education Reaching the Poor

Private education in developing countries isn't just about the poor, of course, and there are many exciting examples of big education chains throughout the developing world, some with as many as 500,000 students in franchised campuses across a region (see Tooley 1999 for more details). But even these big education companies have implications for the ways in which the private sector can reach the least advantaged. Two examples from India can help illustrate this.

An Indian company which embodies much of the excitement and innovation in the education industry is NIIT. With its competitor, Aptech, it shares just over 70 percent of the IT education and training market in India, estimated at roughly 1.1 billion rupees. NIIT has 40 wholly owned centres in the metropolitan areas and about 1,000 franchised centres across India. It also has a global reach, with centres in the US, Asia-Pacific, Europe, Japan, Central Asia, and Africa. A key aspect of NIIT's educational philosophy is that there is a need to harness research to improve the efficiency of learning and to raise educational standards.

Because of NIIT's success in developing innovative and cost-effective IT education and training, several state governments are looking to it—and similar companies—to help bring IT education to the poor in their states. First off the mark was Tamil Nadu, which wanted to bring a computer curriculum to all of its high schools. Significantly, although it allocated extra funds to this endeavour—about US $22 million over 5 years—it simply didn't trust handing the funds over to government schools, perhaps having taken to heart the lessons of the PROBE report. Instead, it developed a model to contract out the delivery to private companies, who provide the software and hardware, while the government provides an electricity supply and the classroom. For the first round of the Tamil Nadu process, 43 contracts were awarded for 666 schools, with NIIT allotted 371 schools. Many of the classrooms have become NIIT centres, open to the school children and teachers during the day, then used by the franchise holder in the evenings. This contracting out of curriculum areas represents an important step forward in relationships between the public and private sectors, and provides an interesting model worth watching and emulating.

Moreover, NIIT has embarked on another endeavour, which has the potential to link the poorest in society to the "knowledge society." We've noted that NIIT is engaged in research and development. One aspect of this has recently focused on how to reach largely illiterate and unschooled children in the slums and rural areas through the Internet. As background, NIIT's Director of Research, Dr. Sugata Mitra experienced what many proud parents feel when he observed his children on the family computer: "My children have easily taught themselves to access the Internet. They must be brilliant!:" Just like their father, perhaps. But then he mused: "Perhaps there's nothing special about my children, but there's something particularly *easy* about accessing the Internet?" Thus was born the "Hole in the Wall" experiment.

Usefully, the NIIT headquarters borders the slum area of Kalkaji, where there are a large number of children of all ages who don't attend school—in any case the only schools available have few resources, and high teacher and pupil absenteeism. Dr. Mitra wondered, Can these children also learn to access the Internet without any tuition?

His research team constructed an "Internet kiosk" in the NIIT boundary wall, with the monitor visible through a glass plate built into the wall. The PC itself was on the other side of the brick enclosure, which was connected to the NIIT's internal network. The kiosk had access to the Internet through a dedicated connection to a service provider. There was a touch pad provided instead of a mouse, which was later modified to an unbreakable joystick. The kiosk was made operational, without any announcement or instruction, in January 1999. A video camera recorded activity near the kiosk and activity was monitored from another PC on the network.

To cut a long story short, within weeks, the children quickly learned to become Internet literate. The children visited websites without any instruction. The Disney Web site became especially popular, with children playing computer games, and navigating stories and cartoons. Those literate in Hindi also loved to access news, horoscopes, and short story sites. Paint also became very popular, with almost all of the 80 children who came to the kiosk learning—without instruction—to make pictures or to write their own names. These are children who wouldn't have access to actual paint and paper.

The observations thus far indicate that underprivileged children from the slum area, without any planned instructional intervention, could achieve a remarkable level of computer literacy. The experiment suggests that language, technical skills, and education are not serious barriers to accessing the Internet, and, through this, educational and entertainment CD ROMs, but instead can lead to self- and peer-education—at least for younger children. Over the age of 14 or so, people didn't make much sense of it all: "Where's the teacher?" they would ask.

Now, if this was just a simple experiment conducted by a company it might not be so spectacular. But the important point is that Dr. Mitra is now embarking on rolling out the idea commercially to rural and slum areas, harnessing the power of the private sector to reach the poorest through modern technology.

Conclusions

When I present my work about the "private alternative" in education at conferences and seminars (see Tooley 2000a), a response I sometimes get from even those who are somewhat sympathetic to my work is along the lines of "It might work for the middle classes, but certainly not for the poor. And what about the poor countries? It certainly wouldn't work for them." No, it is generally assumed that if it is the poor we are concerned about, educationally speaking, then there is no role for the private sector, and its promotion would only be detrimental to their chances.

This chapter has explored this issue by looking at the situation of some of the poorest people in the world, in the slums and villages of India. For these people, it was shown that the government education system is severely malfunctioning. That's not just my view; the government's own sponsored research backs up this hypothesis. The response of many public schools to the poor seems to be at best one of cavalier indifference. On the other hand, partly in response to the perceived inadequacies of state schools, entrepreneurs have set up private schools to serve these poor communities. The PROBE research found these schools were doing much better than the government schools in terms of teacher commitment and teaching time. And other research, both from India and from other developing countries, suggests that private education in general is more effective (at least in terms of student achievement in key subjects), even when controlled for socio-economic class and the background variables of students. Moreover, research from India shows that private (unaided) education is also dramatically more cost-effective than government education.

All this evidence suggests to me that the received wisdom about the role of the private sector in helping the disadvantaged is completely misguided. In developing countries, it is not the state that has the greatest potential to help the poor, but the private sector. Sure, the very poorest may need additional assistance to help them attend these schools, in terms of public or private vouchers (or both). But the state's major role should be to help ensure that the regulatory and investment climate is conducive to the development and nurturing of these schools. And if this is true for India, then it may also be true for the developed world too.

References

James, Estelle. 1991 "Private Higher Education: The Philippines as a Prototype." *Higher Education* 21: 189-206.

Jimenez, Emmanuel, Marlaine Lockheed, and Nongnuch Wattanawaha. 1988. "The Relative Efficiency of Private and Public Schools: The Case of Thailand." *The World Bank Economic Review* 2, no. 2: 139-164.

Jimenez, Emmanuel, Marlaine E. Lockheed, and Vicente Paqueo. 1991. "The Relative Efficiency of Private and Public Schools in Developing Countries" *World Bank Research Observer*. 6, no. 2 (July): 205-218.

Larrañaga, Oswaldo. 1997. "Chile: A Hybrid Approach." In Zuckerman, Elaine, and Emanuel de Kadt, eds., *The Public-private Mix in Social Services: Health Care and Education in Chile, Costa Rica and Venezuela*. Washington DC: Inter-American Development Bank.

Kingdon, Geeta. 1996a. "The Quality and Efficiency of Private and Public Education: A Case Study of Urban India." *Oxford Bulletin of Economics and Statistics* 58.1: 57-81.

Kingdon, Geeta. 1996b. "Private Schooling in India: Size, Nature and Equity-effects." LSE, Development Economics Programme.

Probe Team. 1999. *Public Report on Basic Education in India*. Oxford: Oxford University Press.

Robertson, Heather-Jane. 1998. *No More Teachers, No More Books: The Commercialization of Canada's Schools*. Toronto: McClelland & Stewart.

Tooley, James. 1999. *The Global Education Industry*. London: IEA/IFC.

Tooley, James. 2000a. *Reclaiming Education*. London: Continuum/Cassell.

Tooley, James. 2000b. The Private Sector Serving the Educational Needs of the Poor: A Case Study from India, with Policy Recommendations. Paper for the Public-Private Partnerships in Education Program, Asian Development Bank Institute. Tokyo: 29 May–7 June 2000.

Notes

1   "Reform of Public Education: Lessons from the Developed and Developing World" C*f*BT Education Services Annual Debate, The Royal Commonwealth Society, London, 14th June 1999.
2   In rural India about two-thirds of the population live in that population range.
3   In India, there are also private aided schools, which get the great majority of funding from government, and which are almost indistinguishable from government schools in many respects.
4   These figures need to be taken, of course, in the context of India's poverty. GNP per capita, 1999, is US $450. However, perhaps the most useful point of comparison is to note that there are elite private schools in Andhra Pradesh that charge about US $1,100 per student per year. And the middle range private schools serving senior civil servants, businessmen, etc., charge between US $350-$400 per year.
5   I have just obtained funding to conduct a research and development project along these lines.

Grassroots Perspectives on Market Mechanisms

A Parent's Perspective on School Choice

BARBARA LEWIS,
Scholarship Parent, Indianapolis

What I can tell you about school choice is that, if it hadn't been there, I don't know what I would have done. When I was young, my family sacrificed to put me through private, Catholic school education, and I had always hoped to send my children to one. But being a single mom, I couldn't afford it. All my children started school in the public system. I got discouraged when, one by one, I saw they were not getting the education they deserved.

My oldest son, Alphonso, had always loved school and learning. As a little boy, he attended the federal Head Start pre-school program and an optional kindergarten class before he started grade school. At home, I worked with him teaching him numbers, ABC's, and tying his shoes. So when he started first grade, he was ready for school.

At the beginning, Alphonso was excited about school, but slowly his attitude changed and one day he didn't want to go back. He started making up excuses, saying he was sick, or that he didn't want to go to school. It was kind of scary. I saw the light going out of my child's eyes for education. His teachers told me that he was an above average student who wasn't meeting his potential. When his grades slipped, I asked

This chapter is an edited version of the speech Barbara Lewis made at the Fraser Institute Conference, School Choice: Dispelling the Myths and Examining the Evidence, April 1, 2000.

for extra credit work, or any other help to improve his grades, but I got no response.

They constantly said they wanted parents to be concerned, parents who wanted to get involved. Well, they had me. But as much as I went to the school and tried to get help, I was shut out. They didn't want me there asking questions. "What do you want? What are you doing here?" was the response I got. I replied, "You asked for someone concerned. You asked me to be here. I'm trying to support the teachers; I'm trying to get help for my child."

I heard about the Educational CHOICE Charitable Trust from a co-worker. I applied for it and got a voucher for Alphonso. He used the voucher to get a place at Holy Cross Central Catholic. The first few months weren't easy for him. There was a lot of discipline to get used to, and that was new for him. But once he settled in, his grades stabilized and his attitude changed. He was happy, and he made friends. Everyone around him wanted to learn, just like he did, and that made me happy. What also made me happy was the school was right down the street; he got to walk to school every day with friends in his neighbourhood. His brother and sister got to go to the same school, too. They all got to walk to school together and have the same friends, in the same neighbourhood.

When our family moved from the inner city to the suburbs I got another perspective on the public school system. We moved to Lawrence township when Alphonso was a sophomore in high school and my other two children were still in Holy Cross Central Catholic School. I did a lot of research on the public schools in the area. All the literature said they had great public schools: they had a great curriculum, students did well, and because they were public schools they were free. When we moved I was happy that my two younger kids could go to these public schools that were so highly regarded. Alphonso had been accepted to one of the best high schools in Indiana, a college preparatory school called Cathedral High School, so I sent him there and he is doing very well. I felt confident about sending my daughter, who had had A's and B's at Holy Cross, to the suburban public school.

On the first parents' evening, I visited the school and met the teachers for all her classes. I remember going to each class and giving every one of her teachers three phone numbers: my home phone number, my work phone number and my cell phone number. "If anything is wrong, if Erika steps out of line, if she doesn't turn homework in, you'll be able to reach me," I told them. "There is an answering machine on each and every one of those phone lines."

Erika's first semester was fine; she got her usual A's and B's. But when she brought home her second semester report card I was totally shocked. I didn't understand how a student could go from A's and B's in one semester to straight F's in the next. It took me thirty days to contact the teachers and set up meetings with them all. I reminded them that before she came to this school, I had come to each one of them and given them numbers to call me. I hadn't received one call. No one had told me that homework hadn't been turned in; no one had told me she was misbehaving.

What got me after that—after I tried to get help from the teachers to no avail—was that their next step was to suspend Erika. When they suspended her, I went back to them again and I said, "Okay, we know there is a problem because there is no discipline for Erika. She knows she's going to get away with misbehaving because you're not going to call me. If you did call me I could get her straightened out. We could fix the problem. But instead of helping her and helping me get her grades back to where they were, your solution is to put her out of school for two weeks, which is going to put her behind even more."

Well, they didn't really care about that logic. They had no answer for it. Those were their rules, their guidelines, so this pattern continued. I waited until the end of her sixth-grade year, Erika's first year at that school. All through the year I told my daughter, "If you don't straighten up, you're not going to pass. You've got straight F's on your report card. There's no way they're going to pass you. You're going to be in summer school and you're going to miss your summer."

When the end of the year came, I had no letter from the school about summer school, and I had nothing from the school saying she had to repeat the year. So I called the school. I said, "I'm just checking to see if Erika Lewis has summer school this year or if she's going to the seventh grade." And they checked and said that yes, she had been assigned a seventh grade counsellor.

I said, "Excuse me, but my daughter has straight F's on her report card. How can she have a seventh grade counsellor?"

"Well, she's being promoted to the seventh grade," they said.

"How can that be?" I asked. "How can you promote a child with straight F's on her report card?"

"Well, she passed her IStep test last September," they told me.

"But the IStep test was in the beginning of the year."

"Well, that's what we go by," they said.

So there was nothing that they cared about during the rest of the year. She could have stayed home for the whole year after the IStep test and she would have passed.

We went through this for a year and a half, and at that point, I had had enough. I decided to move my daughter to a private school. Just this week, as a matter of fact, I got her into St. Andrew's Catholic School. I no longer have my choice voucher but things have gone well for me in my career and now I can make that choice on my own for my children. And after all the problems with the schools and realizing that no matter what I do or what my child does, they're going to keep passing her, whether she can read or whether she can write, or whether she has any chance for a good life at all. They don't care about her.

Their excuse is that they've got about 300 kids in the seventh grade and they can't watch all the kids, they say. I told them that I wasn't asking them to watch all the kids, just one. I said, "If you're marking their grades you must know there is something wrong. She went from an A to an F, so give a parent a call or send a letter. Do *something*."

She just started St. Andrew's Catholic School this week and already I have seen an amazing transformation in her. I dropped Erika off Thursday for her first day of school, and for the first time when I picked her up, I saw a smile on her face. I asked her how her first day had been and she said she was happy. She said the kids were all nice. The new school is small and the students are all really close. They were really nice to her and tried to make her feel comfortable and welcome. Everyone in the school felt that way; they made her feel special and feel that she belonged somewhere. And, just as importantly, she knows there are rules that she has to follow now.

Parents know what's best for their children, and we need the opportunity to choose what's right for them. If a school is too big, if a school is too violent or teachers don't understand what is going on in the children's lives, parents need the opportunity to make a change. They need to be able to send their children to a school they feel will be better for them. And with the organization I started, called FORCE, that's what we're trying to get Indiana legislators to see.

If you have any doubts about the quality of public and private schools, I suggest you go and look at a few. Maybe that will give you insight into what's going on in them and how much parents need your help. If it weren't for school choice, I don't know where my oldest son would be or where my daughter would be headed. Alphonso has come such a long way. He wants to go to Notre Dame College and he's got a career plan. In Catholic School they teach him confidence, they teach him that he can do even better than he is doing right now. That is all I want for my children. And that's my perspective on school choice.

A Student's Perspective on School Vouchers

ALPHONSO HARRELL,
Scholarship Student, Indianapolis

I would like to begin by thanking everyone for having me here to tell you about my experiences in public school and private Catholic schools.

When I was in public school I felt like I was being denied something and was not living up to my full potential. The problem was that nobody at school cared whether I learned anything there or not. My mother saw there was a problem and applied for a voucher from the Educational CHOICE Trust so I could go to another school.

When I won the voucher and started at Holy Cross, things were very different and I didn't like it. I was the only minority in my class. There were fourteen or fifteen people in the class, and I was the only Black student. As I say, I didn't like it. There was more discipline. At public school, they let us know that if we showed up, we'd probably pass. At Catholic school, we had to earn our grades, and I wasn't used to that. But as the year went on, the school grew on me and I started to see that the teachers really cared about us. I started making new friends, I started doing better in school, and I started liking it. School was pretty much the main thing in my life. I liked going to school, and I didn't like the summer holidays any more because I didn't get to see my friends.

This chapter is an edited version of the speech Alphonso Harrell made at the Fraser Institute Conference, School Choice: Dispelling the Myths and Examining the Evidence, April 1, 2000.

As the year went on I got on the honour roll, which I had never made in public school. Now I am in eleventh grade and I look at my old friends in the same grade in public school and I see a huge difference between us. I mean, they're down on one level and I'm way up on another. They can barely do the math that I do. They're in beginning math, Algebra 1, and I'm going into Algebra 2. If I transferred back into a public school next year with all the credits I've earned and all the extra-curricular activities I've done, I would only have to take two classes a day, and I would graduate half a year earlier than everybody else.

These things that I have accomplished, I've done because of two people: Mr. Rooney, who started the Educational CHOICE Charitable Trust, which paid for my school voucher, and the main person in my life, my Mom. I don't know where I would be if she hadn't made the choice to put me in this program.

I think there are a couple of things a kid needs to get by in life. The first thing a kid needs is a parent who cares, a parent who asks you every day how you're doing in school. "What kind of grades are you getting? How do you like your teachers?" my Mom would ask me. I'd usually answer her saying something like, "I don't know, I'm doing okay," the usual answers. But I always knew somebody cared and that helped me do a little bit better. And the other thing a kid needs is for a teacher to care enough to put up with you even though you might not be on your best behaviour or having your best day. The teacher and the school have to look out for you. Most teachers have the attitude that they'll come to school and teach the students who want to learn. If you don't want to learn, you just need to show up to class and the teachers will pass you anyway.

That's not how it is in Catholic School. If you don't want to learn, the teachers call your parents, they talk to the principal, and they talk to you. They stay on top of you. They didn't let me fall through the cracks, the way they did in public school. I almost fell through the cracks but luckily I had a Mom who cared enough to make sure I got the education I needed. Now I'm in high school, preparing for college, and I see my friends who are preparing to work at Burger King for the rest of their lives.

I love all the opportunities that I get to speak about my experiences because it gives other people hope. They can see that an ordinary kid from public school who was not doing well can get a better education just by going to a private school. Now, because of CHOICE, I've got a chance to excel at one of the best high schools in Indianapolis and a whole bunch of doors are suddenly open for me. I can go to just about any college I want in Indiana just because I go to this school. My school cares about grades. They can kick you out just for not having a 2.0, which is a "C" average. That motivates us to work a little harder.

Another good thing about my school is that I can go to school without worrying all the time. Am I going to get beaten up? No. Do I have to worry about getting shot at school? No. Do I have to go through a metal detector? No. At public school the kids do worry about that kind of thing. They don't worry about what kind of homework they have; they worry about what's going to happen to them after school because they're not safe. I'm in a safe environment so I can put more energy into my grades and extracurricular activities instead of worrying about what's going to happen to me after school.

And finally, I'd like to say that when you have someone who cares about you, even just one person, it can make a real difference for you. You just have to let students know that you care because if a kid feels that nobody out there cares about him, he'll lose self-esteem and maybe he might do something just to get your attention. We say, "Knock, knock, is anybody home? Is anyone paying attention to me?" If the answer had been no, for me, I'd probably be in trouble right now and not on my school's Honour Roll.

If, however, everybody had the experience that I had in public school and Catholic school, and could choose between them, I guarantee everybody would choose the Catholic school. I have been at many school CHOICE lotteries where half the parents in public school came to try to win a voucher to get their kids into a private school. If public school is so much better than a private school, then why are all these parents trying to pull their kids out and put them into a private school?

Public schools get so much more money than any of the private schools I know, and the private schools are doing a much better job for students. It doesn't make sense. So instead of wasting money on a public school, trying to help a losing cause, you should help a winning cause and give more money to private schools.

And that's my speech.